Lumos Test Mastery
Grade 5 English Practice

Online Access

Get the login details from your teacher and write them in the box below.

Login details for online access.

Table of Contents

Online Access		1

Chapter 1	**Reading Literature**		4
Lesson 1	Supporting Statements		5
Lesson 2	Drawing Inferences		11
Lesson 3	Theme		21
Lesson 4	Characters		30
Lesson 5	Summarizing Texts		39
Lesson 6	Events		51
Lesson 7	Setting		61
Lesson 8	Figurative Language		69
Lesson 9	Structures of Text		74
Lesson 10	Styles of Narration		80
Lesson 11	Visual Elements		86
Lesson 12	Compare and Contrast		90

Chapter 2	**Reading Informational Text**		96
Lesson 1	Inferences and Conclusions		97
Lesson 2	Main Idea and Supporting Details		100
Lesson 3	Text Relationships		106
Lesson 4	General Academic Vocabulary		111
Lesson 5	Text Structure		114
Lesson 6	Point of View		117
Lesson 7	Locating Answers		120
Lesson 8	Using Evidence to Support Claims		123
Lesson 9	Integrating Information		128

Chapter 3	Language	131
Lesson 1	Pronoun-Antecedent Agreement	132
Lesson 2	Prepositional phrases	135
Lesson 3	Verbs	138
Lesson 4	Subject verb agreement	141
Lesson 5	Adjectives & Adverbs	144
Lesson 6	Correlative conjunctions	147
Lesson 7	Capitalization	150
Lesson 8	Punctuation	153
Lesson 9	Commas in Introductory phrases	155
Lesson 10	Using commas	157
Lesson 11	Writing titles	159
Lesson 12	Spelling	162
Lesson 13	Sentence structure	165
Lesson 14	Varieties in English	169
Lesson 15	Multiple-Meaning Words	171
Lesson 16	Context clues	173
Lesson 17	Roots & Affixes	177
Lesson 18	Reference sources	180
Lesson 19	Interpreting figurative language	183
Lesson 20	Idioms, Adages & Proverbs	186
Lesson 21	Synonyms & Antonyms	189
Lesson 22	Vocabulary	192
Copyright		**195**

Chapter 1
Reading Literature

Do NOT write your answers in this book. To open the answer sheet, scan the QR code or visit **lumoslearning.com/a/5e001**

Lesson 1: Supporting Statements

Question 1 is based on the poem below

What is this life if, full of care,
We have no time to stand and stare?

No time to stand beneath the boughs
And stare as long as sheep or cows.

No time to see, when woods we pass,
Where squirrels hide their nuts in grass

No time to see, in broad daylight,
Streams full of stars, like skies at night.

No time to turn at Beauty's glance,
And watch her feet, how they can dance.

No time to wait till her mouth can
Enrich that smile her eyes began.

A poor life if, full of care,
We have no time to stand and stare.

-- W. H. Davies

1. Where can you find the answer to the question in the first stanza?

Ⓐ In the first stanza
Ⓑ In the fourth stanza
Ⓒ In the last stanza
Ⓓ The poet does not answer the question

Question 2-7 are based on the story below

After reading the story, enter the details in the map below. This will help you to answer the questions that follow.

Once there was a severe drought. There was little water in Tony's well, and he didn't know what would happen to the fruit trees in his garden. Just then, he noticed three men looking intently at his house. He was certain that the three strangers were planning to rob his house. He acted quickly. He shouted out to his son, "My son, due to the drought, money has become scarce. There are many thieves. Let us protect our valuables, and put all of our jewels in a box and throw them into the well. They will be safe there." He quickly told his son to put some large stones in a box and throw them into the well. The thieves heard the sound of the box falling into the well and were happy.

That night they came to the well. The box was heavy and had landed deep down in the well. To get it, they would have to take out some of the water. They started drawing water from the well and pouring it onto the ground. Tony had made arrangements to make sure that the water reached his fruit trees. He had channels leading from the well to each of the trees.

By the time thieves found the box, they had drawn out enough water to water the trees. It was almost dawn. Tony sent for the soldiers, and just as the thieves were trying to open the box, they were caught red-handed.

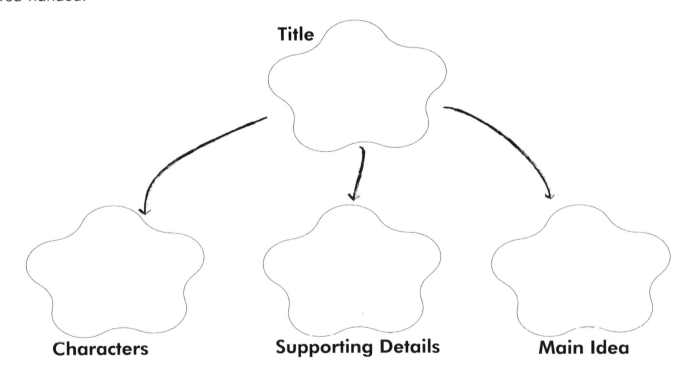

2. What would be an appropriate title for the story?

   Ⓐ "Cunning Tony"
   Ⓑ "The Thieves"
   Ⓒ "The Well"
   Ⓓ "A Clever Idea"

3. What did Tony secretly ask his son to do?

   Ⓐ To put the clothes in the box
   Ⓑ To put the jewels in the box
   Ⓒ To put the papers in the box
   Ⓓ To put large stones in the box

4. The fruit trees got enough water because_____.

   Ⓐ The thieves drew the water from the well and poured it onto the ground.
   Ⓑ The thieves did not draw the water from the well.
   Ⓒ The thieves watered the garden.
   Ⓓ Tony watered the garden.

5. What happened to the thieves as they were trying to open the box?

   Ⓐ They found the jewels.
   Ⓑ They were caught red-handed.
   Ⓒ They did not find the box.
   Ⓓ They took the money.

6. What is the main purpose of the first paragraph in the story?

   Ⓐ It introduces us to the story and the characters in the story.
   Ⓑ It introduces us to the situation in the story.
   Ⓒ It lays the setting or the foundation for the story.
   Ⓓ All of the above

7. Which detail in the story tells us that the country was going through a difficult time?

   Ⓐ Once there was a severe drought.
   Ⓑ There was little water in Tony's well.
   Ⓒ He shouted out to his son, "My son, because of the drought, money has become scarce."
   Ⓓ All of the above

Question 8-10 are based on the story below

After reading the story, enter the details in the map below. This will help you to answer the questions that follow.

The Glass Cupboard

There was a king who had a cupboard that was made entirely of glass. It was a special cupboard. It looked empty, but you could always take out anything you wanted. There was only one thing that had to be remembered. Whenever something was taken out of it, something else had to be put back in, although nobody knew why.

One day some thieves broke into the palace and stole the cupboard. "Now, we can have anything we want," they said. One of the thieves said, "I want a large bag of gold," and he opened the glass cupboard and got it. The other two did the same, and they, too, got exactly what they wanted. The thieves forgot one thing. Not one of them put anything back inside the cupboard.

This went on and on for weeks and months. At last, the leader of the thieves could bear it no longer. He took a hammer and smashed the glass cupboard into a million pieces, and then all three thieves fell down dead.

When the king returned home, he ordered his servants to search for the cupboard. When the servants found it and the dead thieves, they filled sixty great carts with the gold and took it back to the king. He said, "If those thieves had only put something back into the cupboard, they would be alive to this day."

He ordered his servants to collect all of the pieces of glass and melt into a globe of the world with all the countries on it; this was to remind himself and others, to give back something in return when someone shows an act of kindness or gives us something

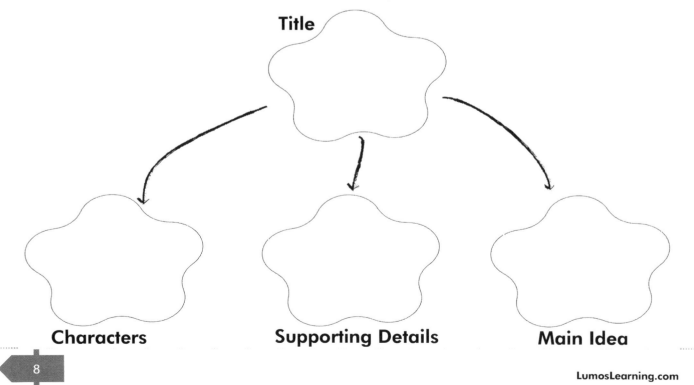

8. What happened when the king was away?

Ⓐ There was a storm, and it smashed the glass cupboard.
Ⓑ The people in the palace accidentally broke the glass cupboard.
Ⓒ Some thieves broke into the palace and stole the glass cupboard.
Ⓓ None of the above

9. What did the thieves take out of the cupboard?

Ⓐ They took out bags of gold.
Ⓑ They took out bags of silver.
Ⓒ They took out bags of diamonds.
Ⓓ They took out bags of stones.

10. What did the thieves forget to do?

Ⓐ They forgot to take out everything that was in the cupboard every time.
Ⓑ They forgot to break the cupboard each time they took something out.
Ⓒ They forgot to take out the jewels.
Ⓓ They forgot to put something back each time they took something out.

Question 11 is based on the story below

After reading the story, enter the details in the map below. This will help you to answer the questions that follow.

The Traveler

A weary traveler stopped at Sam's house and asked him for shelter for the night. Sam was a friendly soul. He not only agreed to let the traveler stay for the night; he decided to treat his guest to some curried chicken. So he bought a couple of chickens from the market and gave them to his wife to cook. Then he went off to buy some fruit.

Now Sam's wife could not resist food. She had a habit of eating as she cooked. So, as she cooked the meat, she smelled the rich steam and could not help tasting a piece. It was tender and delicious, and she decided to have another piece. Soon there was only a tiny bit left. Her little son, Kevin, ran into the kitchen. She gave him that little piece.

Kevin found it so tasty that he begged his mother for more. But there was no more chicken left. The traveler, who had gone to have a wash, returned. The woman heard him coming and had to think of a plan quickly. She began to scold her son loudly. "Your father has taught you a shameful and disgusting habit. Stop it, I tell you!" The traveler was curious. "What habit has his father taught the child?" he asked.
"Oh," said the woman, "Whenever a guest arrives, my husband cuts off their ears and roasts them for my son to eat."

The traveler was shocked. He picked up his shoes and fled.

"Why has our guest left in such a hurry?" asked Sam when he came back.

"A fine guest indeed!" exclaimed his wife. "He snatched the chickens out of my pot and ran off with them!"

"The chickens!" exclaimed Sam. He ran after his guest, shouting. "Let me have one, at least; you may keep the other!" But his guest only ran faster!

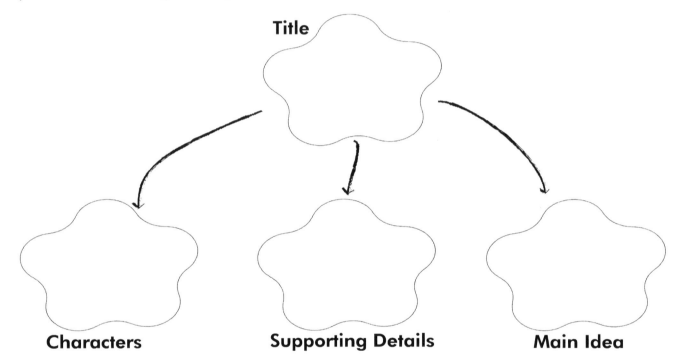

11. Part A

   Why did Sam run after the guest?

   Ⓐ Sam wanted the traveler's ears.
   Ⓑ Sam wanted the traveler's shoes.
   Ⓒ Sam wanted the guest to stay.
   Ⓓ Sam wanted one of his chickens.

   Part B

   Which details in the above paragraph support the fact that the traveler was scared?

   Ⓐ The traveler was curious.
   Ⓑ The traveler was shocked. He picked up his shoes and fled.
   Ⓒ The traveler, who had gone to have a wash, returned.
   Ⓓ None of the above.

Do NOT write your answers in this book. To open the answer sheet, scan the QR code or visit *lumoslearning.com/a/5e002*

Chapter 1 → Lesson 2: Drawing Inferences

Question 1 and 3 are based on the story below

After reading the story, enter the details in the map. This will help you to answer the questions that follow.

A Clever Idea

Once there was a severe drought. There was little water in Tony's well, and he didn't know what would happen to the fruit trees in his garden. Just then, he noticed three men looking intently at his house. He was certain that the three strangers were planning to rob his house. He acted quickly. He shouted out to his son, "My son, due to the drought, money has become scarce. There are many thieves. Let us protect our valuables, and put all of our jewels in a box and throw them into the well. They will be safe there." He quickly told his son to put some large stones in a box and throw them into the well. The thieves heard the sound of the box falling into the well and were happy.

That night they came to the well. The box was heavy and had landed deep down in the well. To get it, they would have to take out some of the water. They started drawing water from the well and pouring it onto the ground. Tony had made arrangements to make sure that the water reached his fruit trees. He had channels leading from the well to each of the trees.

By the time thieves found the box, they had drawn out enough water to water the trees. It was almost dawn. Tony sent for the soldiers, and just as the thieves were trying to open the box, they were caught red-handed.

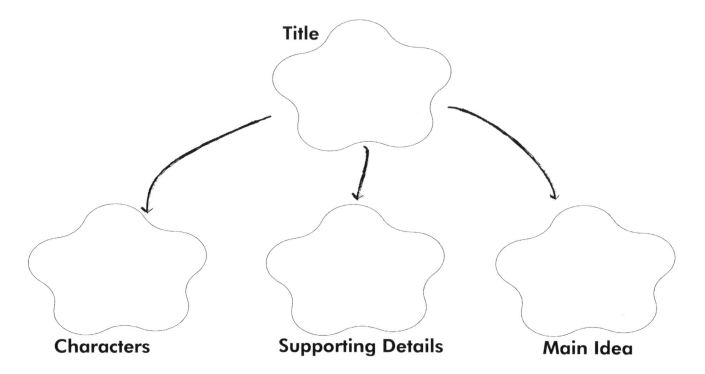

1. The above passage is about _____.

   Ⓐ how the thieves watered the field
   Ⓑ how the thieves robbed for money
   Ⓒ how the thieves took the jewels
   Ⓓ how the thieves put the box in the well

2. Why did Tony throw a box of stones down the well?

   Ⓐ The stones were valuable to Tony.
   Ⓑ The stones were worth a fortune.
   Ⓒ The stones were a diversion.
   Ⓓ There was no money at all.

3. Why did Tony send for soldiers?

   Ⓐ Tony worked for the Army.
   Ⓑ They enforced the laws of the area.
   Ⓒ The police were stealing the jewels.
   Ⓓ Tony trusted the thieves.

Question 4 and 5 are based on the story below

After reading the story, enter the details in the map. This will help you to answer the questions that follow.

The Traveler

A weary traveler stopped at Sam's house and asked him for shelter for the night. Sam was a friendly soul. He not only agreed to let the traveler stay for the night; and he decided to treat his guest to some curried chicken. So he bought a couple of chickens from the market and gave them to his wife to cook. Then, he went off to buy some fruit.

Now, Sam's wife could not resist food. She had a habit of eating as she cooked. So as she cooked the meat, she smelled the rich steam and could not help tasting a piece. It was tender and delicious, and she decided to have another piece. Soon, there was only a tiny bit left.

Her little son, Kevin, ran into the kitchen. She gave him that little piece. Kevin found it so tasty that he begged his mother for more. But, there was no more chicken left. The traveler, who had gone to have a wash, returned. The woman heard him coming and had to think of a plan quickly. She began to scold her son loudly: "Your father has taught you a shameful and disgusting habit. Stop it, I tell you!"

The traveler was curious. "What habit has his father taught the child?" he asked.

"Oh," said the woman, "Whenever a guest arrives, my husband cuts off their ears and roasts them for my son to eat."

The traveler was shocked. He picked up his shoes and fled. "Why has our guest left in such a hurry?" asked Sam when he came back.

"A fine guest indeed!" exclaimed his wife. "He snatched the chickens out of my pot and ran off with them!"

"The chickens!" exclaimed Sam. He ran after his guest, shouting, "Let me have one, at least; you may keep the other!" But, his guest only ran faster!

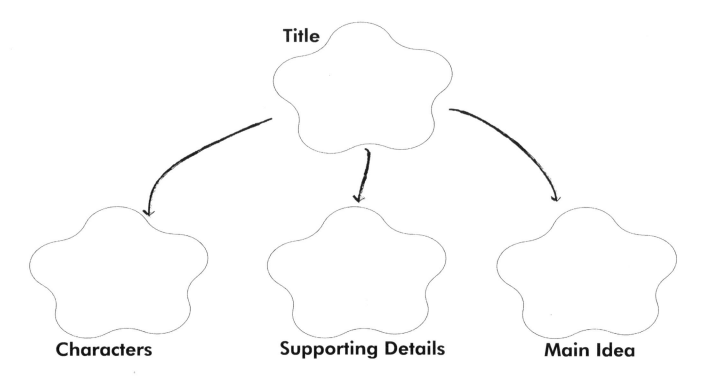

4. According to the above story, what kind of a man was Sam?

   Ⓐ He was a friendly and helpful man.
   Ⓑ He was a dangerous and cruel man.
   Ⓒ He was a miserly and cunning man.
   Ⓓ He was a friendly and miserable man.

5. According to the above story, how can you describe the character of Sam's wife?

   Ⓐ She liked food a lot.
   Ⓑ She was very cunning and clever.
   Ⓒ She was a very good cook.
   Ⓓ All of the above

Question 6-9 are based on the story below

After reading the story, enter the details in the map below. This will help you to answer the questions that follow.

Do Your Best

Katie stood before the crowd, blushing and wringing her hands. She looked out and saw the room full of faces. Some she knew, and some she did not. But, they were all here to listen to her. Taking a deep breath, she opened her mouth, but no words came out. Tears formed in the corners of her eyes as she closed them.

With her eyes closed, she imagined her mother helping her get dressed and ready for tonight. "Just do your best," is what her mother had told her.

She opened her eyes and found her mother's smiling face in the crowd. Relaxing, she took another deep breath and started singing. She did not stop until she finished, and the crowd was on their feet applauding.

After the show, she found her parents and her friends. They all had wonderful things to say about her song and how proud they were because she kept going even when it seemed like she might give up. She shrugged her shoulders and shared a smile with her mother.

"I just did my best," she answered.

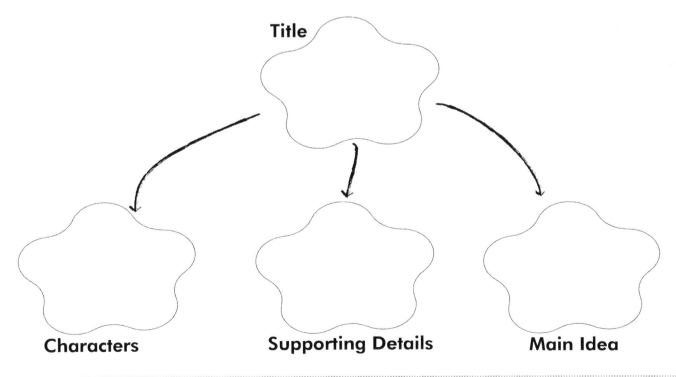

6. The above passage is about _____.

Ⓐ being determined
Ⓑ giving up
Ⓒ listening to friends
Ⓓ taking a deep breath

7. At the beginning of the story, how was Katie feeling?

Ⓐ Katie was friendly.
Ⓑ Katie was excited.
Ⓒ Katie was depressed.
Ⓓ Katie was nervous.

8. At the beginning of the show, what did Katie's friends think she would do?

Ⓐ Stand there or walk off the stage
Ⓑ Sing a beautiful song
Ⓒ Her friends were not paying attention
Ⓓ None of the above

9. What does the author hope to accomplish in the second paragraph?

Ⓐ The author wants the reader to see how nervous Katie is.
Ⓑ The author wants the reader to see where Katie gets her strength.
Ⓒ The author wants the reader to see why Katie gives up.
Ⓓ The author wants the reader to see how silly Katie is being.

Question 10 is based on the poem below

What is this life if, full of care,
We have no time to stand and stare?

No time to stand beneath the boughs
And stare as long as sheep or cows.

No time to see, when woods we pass,
Where squirrels hide their nuts in grass

No time to see, in broad daylight,
Streams full of stars, like skies at night.

No time to turn at Beauty's glance,
And watch her feet, how they can dance.

No time to wait till her mouth can
Enrich that smile her eyes began.

A poor life if, full of care,
We have no time to stand and stare.

-- W. H. Davies

10. What do you think is an appropriate title for the above poem?

Ⓐ "Stand and Stare"
Ⓑ "Leisure"
Ⓒ "Hard Work"
Ⓓ "No Time"

Question 11 is based on the story below

After reading the story, enter the details in the map below. This will help you to answer the questions that follow.

Late for School

Marrah heard the brakes on the bus as she shoveled the rest of her breakfast into her mouth. "You just missed the bus!" Marrah's mother yelled. "Why can't you ever be on time?"

"I'm sorry, Mom," Marrah sighed. She ran upstairs to her room so she could get her backpack, knowing she needed to hurry because her mother would have to take her to school.

"Let's go, Marrah!" Her mother called from downstairs. "You don't want to be late for school too!"

Frantic now, Marrah lifted her sheets to look under them before dropping to her knees in front of her bed. She pushed mounds of clothes out of the way as she continued to search for her backpack.

"Marrah!" Her mother called again, and she could hear the impatience in her mother's voice downstairs. She ran out of her room and leaned over the rail.

"I can't find my backpack!" She cried out.

"You mean this one?" Her mother pulled the bag from the floor beside her.

"Oh," she replied, her shoulders sagging as she walked down the stairs.

"Let's go to school, Marrah." Her mother said with a small smile on her face as they walked out the door.

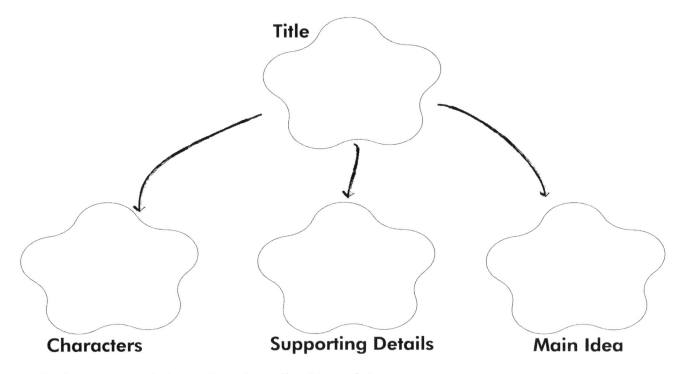

11. **Which characteristics below describe Marrah?**

   Ⓐ Happy, organized, punctual
   Ⓑ Sad, depressed, unhappy
   Ⓒ Disorganized, frustrated, tardy
   Ⓓ Annoyed, confused, pleased

Question 12 is based on the story below

After reading the story, enter the details in the map below. This will help you to answer the questions that follow.

THE LITTLE PINK ROSE

Best Stories to Tell to Children (1912)
By Sara Cone Bryant

Once there was a little pink Rosebud, and she lived down in a little dark house under the ground. One day she was sitting there, all by herself, and it was very still. Suddenly, she heard a little tap, tap, tap, at the door. "Who is that?" she said.

"It's the Rain, and I want to come in," said a soft, sad, little voice.

"No, you can't come in," the little Rosebud said. By and by she heard another little tap, tap, tap, on the windowpane. "Who is there?" she said.

The same soft, little voice answered, "It's the Rain, and I want to come in!"

"No, you can't come in," said the little Rosebud. Then she was very still for a long time. At last, there came a little rustling, whispering sound all around the window? rustle, whisper, whisper. "Who is there?" asked the little Rosebud.

"It's the Sunshine," said a little, soft, cheery voice, "and I want to come in!"

"N -- no," said the little pink rose, "you can't come in." And she sat still again.

Pretty soon, she heard the sweet little rustling noise at the key-hole. "Who is there?" she said.

"It's the Sunshine," said the cheery, little voice, "and I want to come in. I want to come in!"

"No, no," said the little pink rose, "you cannot come in."

By and by, as she sat so still, she heard tap, tap, tap and rustle, whisper, rustle all up and down the windowpane, and on the door, and at the key-hole. "Who is there?" she asked.

"It's the Rain and the Sunshine, the Rain and the Sunshine," said two little voices, together, "and we want to come in! We want to come in! We want to come in!"

"Dear, dear," said the little Rosebud, "if there are two of you, I s'pose I shall have to let you in." So she opened the door a little wee crack, and they came in. And one took one of her little hands, and the other took her other little hand, and they ran, ran, ran with her right up to the top of the ground. Then they said, --

"Poke your head through!"

So she poked her head through, and she was in the midst of a beautiful garden. It was springtime, and all the other flowers had their heads poked through, and she was the prettiest little pink rose in the whole garden!

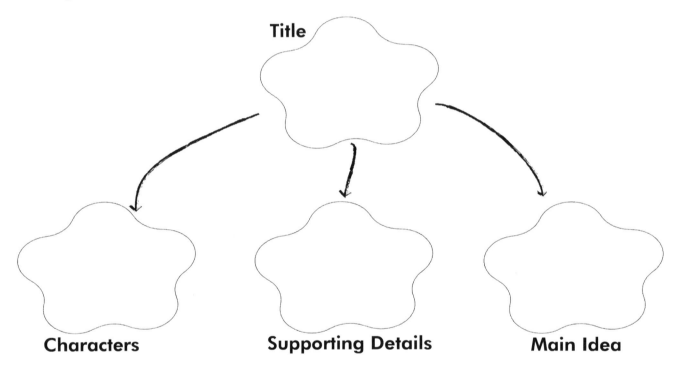

12. What conclusion can you draw from the story?

    Ⓐ Flowers make friends.
    Ⓑ Flowers need the sun and the rain to grow.
    Ⓒ Flowers need other flowers in order to grow.
    Ⓓ Flowers need sunshine in their garden.

Do NOT write your answers in this book. To open the answer sheet, scan the QR code or visit **lumoslearning.com/a/5e003**

Chapter 1 → Lesson 3: Theme

Question 1-3 are based on the story below

After reading the story, enter the details in the map below. This will help you to answer the questions that follow.

Katie stood before the crowd, blushing and wringing her hands. She looked out and saw the room full of faces. Some she knew, and some she did not. But, they were all here to listen to her. Taking a deep breath, she opened her mouth, but no words came out. Tears formed in the corners of her eyes as she closed them.

With her eyes closed, she imagined her mother helping her get dressed and ready for tonight. "Just do your best," is what her mother had told her. She opened her eyes and found her mother's smiling face in the crowd. Relaxing, she took another deep breath and started singing. She did not stop until she finished, and the crowd was on their feet applauding.

After the show, she found her parents and her friends. They all had wonderful things to say about her song and how proud they were because she kept going even when it seemed like she might give up. She shrugged her shoulders and shared a smile with her mother. "I just did my best," she answered.

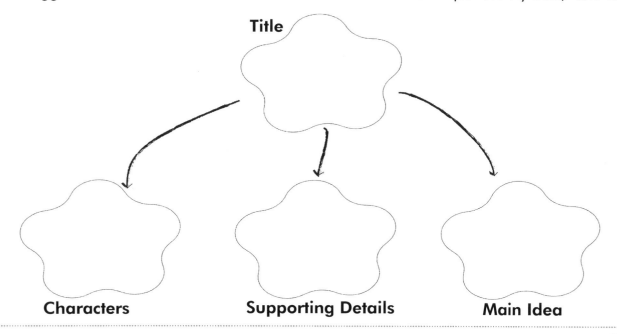

1. **Choose a suitable title for this story.**

   Ⓐ "Trust People"
   Ⓑ "Listening to Mom"
   Ⓒ "Do Your Best"
   Ⓓ "The Show"

2. **What is the overall theme of this story?**

   Ⓐ Give up under pressure.
   Ⓑ Always do your best.
   Ⓒ Never let your friends get you down.
   Ⓓ Close your eyes when you are getting ready to sing.

3. **What can we learn from this story?**

Question 4 is based on the story below

After reading the story, enter the details in the map below. This will help you to answer the questions that follow.

The Glass Cupboard

There was a king who had a cupboard that was made entirely of glass. It was a special cupboard. It looked empty, but you could always take out anything you wanted. There was only one thing that had to be remembered. Whenever something was taken out of it, something else had to be put back in, although nobody knew why.

One day some thieves broke into the palace and stole the cupboard. "Now, we can have anything we want," they said. One of the thieves said, "I want a large bag of gold," and he opened the glass cupboard and got it. The other two did the same, and they, too, got exactly what they wanted. The thieves forgot one thing. Not one of them put anything back inside the cupboard.

This went on and on for weeks and months. At last, the leader of the thieves could bear it no longer. He took a hammer and smashed the glass cupboard into a million pieces, and then all three thieves fell down dead.

When the king returned home, he ordered his servants to search for the cupboard. When the servants found it and the dead thieves, they filled sixty great carts with the gold and took it back to the king. He said, "If those thieves had only put something back into the cupboard, they would be alive to this day."

He ordered his servants to collect all of the pieces of glass and melt into a globe of the world with all the countries on it; this was to remind himself and others, to give back something in return when someone shows an act of kindness or gives us something.

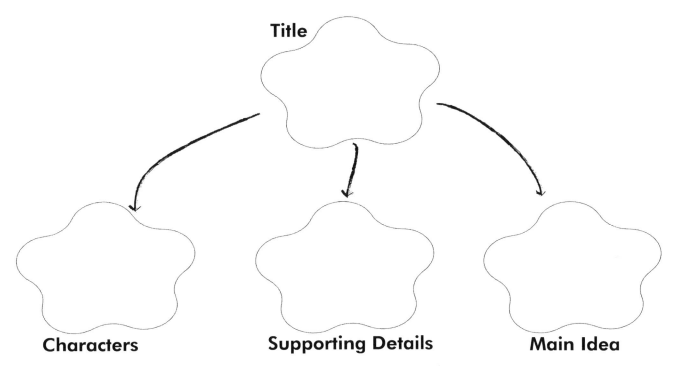

4. What is the purpose of this story?

Ⓐ This story is about learning how to break a glass cupboard.
Ⓑ This story is about learning the importance of gold.
Ⓒ This story is about giving something back in return.
Ⓓ This story is about a king.

Question 5 and 6 are based on the poem below

What is this life if, full of care,
We have no time to stand and stare?

No time to stand beneath the boughs
And stare as long as sheep or cows.

No time to see, when woods we pass,
Where squirrels hide their nuts in grass

No time to see, in broad daylight,
Streams full of stars, like skies at night.

No time to turn at Beauty's glance,
And watch her feet, how they can dance.

No time to wait till her mouth can
Enrich that smile her eyes began.

A poor life if, full of care,
We have no time to stand and stare.

- W. H. Davies

5. What is the poet saying in the last stanza of the poem?

Ⓐ This stanza is saying that life is poor even if you have everything, because you have no time to stand and stare.
Ⓑ This stanza is saying that life is not good.
Ⓒ This stanza is saying that there is no time to stand and stare, so life is good.
Ⓓ None of the above.

6. Choose a suitable title for this poem.

Ⓐ Life
Ⓑ Stare
Ⓒ Stop and Stare
Ⓓ Life and Stare

Question 7 is based on the poem below

My daddy is a tiger,
My mother is a bear

My sister is a pest,
Who messes with my hair

And even though my home,
Is like living in a zoo

I know my family loves me,
And will take care of me too

7. What is this author trying to say in this poem?

Ⓐ Even though the author's family is crazy, they will still take care of each other.
Ⓑ The author's family is too crazy to care.
Ⓒ The author's family is like a bunch of animals.
Ⓓ The author's family is unpredictable.

Question 8 and 9 are based on the poem below

In the kitchen,
After the aimless

Chatter of the plates,
The murmur of the stoves,

The chuckles of the water pipes,
And the sharp exchanges

Of the knives, forks, and spoons,
Comes the serious quiet

When the sink slowly clears its throat,
And you can hear the occasional rumble

Of the refrigerator's tummy
As it digests the cold.

8. Choose a suitable title for this poem.

   Ⓐ "The Sink"
   Ⓑ "The Plates"
   Ⓒ "The Kitchen"
   Ⓓ "The Refrigerator"

9. There is a lot of _____ in this kitchen.

   Ⓐ silence and stillness
   Ⓑ sound and activity
   Ⓒ chatter and murmur
   Ⓓ rumble and chill

Question 10 is based on the paragraph below

Yesterday, I decided to bake a cake. I mixed the ingredients, poured it into a pan, and placed the pan in the oven. Twenty minutes later, I heard the timer ring and I reached into the oven to pull out the cake. I quickly realized that I had forgotten to put oven mitts on! As a result, I ended up with yummy cake but extremely burned hands.

10. What is the theme of the passage?

    Ⓐ Enjoy your cake.
    Ⓑ Have fun baking.
    Ⓒ Be careful when baking.
    Ⓓ Never make a cake.

Question 11 is based on the story below

After reading the story, enter the details in the map below. This will help you to answer the questions that follow.

THE LITTLE PINK ROSE

Best Stories to Tell to Children (1912)
By Sara Cone Bryant

Once there was a little pink Rosebud, and she lived down in a little dark house under the ground. One day she was sitting there, all by herself, and it was very still. Suddenly, she heard a little tap, tap, tap, at the door. "Who is that?" she said.

"It's the Rain, and I want to come in," said a soft, sad, little voice.

"No, you can't come in," the little Rosebud said. By and by she heard another little tap, tap, tap, on the windowpane. "Who is there?" she said.

The same soft, little voice answered, "It's the Rain, and I want to come in!"

"No, you can't come in," said the little Rosebud. Then she was very still for a long time. At last, there came a little rustling, whispering sound all around the window? rustle, whisper, whisper. "Who is there?" asked the little Rosebud.

"It's the Sunshine," said a little, soft, cheery voice, "and I want to come in!"

"N -- no," said the little pink rose, "you can't come in." And she sat still again.

Pretty soon, she heard the sweet little rustling noise at the key-hole. "Who is there?" she said.

"It's the Sunshine," said the cheery, little voice, "and I want to come in. I want to come in!"

"No, no," said the little pink rose, "you cannot come in."

By and by, as she sat so still, she heard tap, tap, tap and rustle, whisper, rustle all up and down the windowpane, and on the door, and at the key-hole. "Who is there?" she asked.

"It's the Rain and the Sunshine, the Rain and the Sunshine," said two little voices, together, "and we want to come in! We want to come in! We want to come in!"

"Dear, dear," said the little Rosebud, "if there are two of you, I s'pose I shall have to let you in." So she opened the door a little wee crack, and they came in. And one took one of her little hands, and the other took her other little hand, and they ran, ran, ran with her right up to the top of the ground.

Then they said, --

"Poke your head through!"

So she poked her head through, and she was in the midst of a beautiful garden. It was springtime, and all the other flowers had their heads poked through, and she was the prettiest little pink rose in the whole garden!

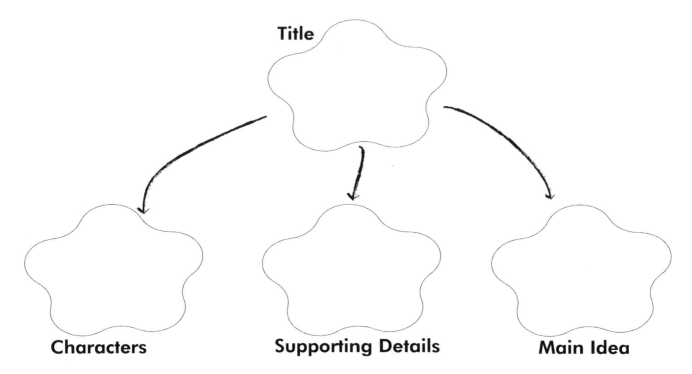

11. What is the theme of the story?

Ⓐ Take a risk and good things may happen.
Ⓑ Do your best.
Ⓒ Do not give up.
Ⓓ Never talk to strangers.

Question 12 is based on the passage below

My mother works extremely hard as a nurse. Each day she gives her all, and when she comes home, she is dog tired. I like to help her take a load off, so I try and make dinner for her. I also clean the house and mow the yard outside. Today was even more difficult, though. It rained like cats and dogs all afternoon, so I couldn't take care of the yard. Then, when I came inside to clean, I realized the kitchen sink was clogged, and the washing machine seemed broken. I couldn't catch a break! By the time Mom came home, I had given up, called a plumber, and ordered a pizza. It's a good thing my mom always taught me that where there is a will, there is a way!

12. What is the overall theme of this passage?

Ⓐ Take the time to be helpful.
Ⓑ Call the plumber if you need to.
Ⓒ You can enjoy pizza when your chores are finished.
Ⓓ Do not let your mother get too busy.

Question 13 is based on the passage below

I went for a run this morning. Although I usually run in the evening, I decided to go in the morning because of the weather. It has been so hot this summer, so hot in fact, that I cannot run in the evening. Therefore, until we have cooler weather, I will continue to enjoy a morning run.

13. What is the overall theme of this passage?

Ⓐ Take the time to run.
Ⓑ Be careful of when you choose to exercise.
Ⓒ Exercise is beneficial.
Ⓓ Enjoy running in the morning.

Do NOT write your answers in this book. To open the answer sheet, scan the QR code or visit **lumoslearning.com/a/5e004**

Chapter 1 → Lesson 4: Characters

After reading the story, enter the details in the map below. This will help you to answer the questions that follow.

A Clever Idea

Once there was a severe drought. There was little water in Tony's well, and he didn't know what would happen to the fruit trees in his garden. Just then, he noticed three men looking intently at his house. He was certain that the three strangers were planning to rob his house. He acted quickly. He shouted out to his son, "My son, due to the drought, money has become scarce. There are many thieves. Let us protect our valuables, and put all of our jewels in a box and throw them into the well. They will be safe there." He quickly told his son to put some large stones in a box and throw them into the well. The thieves heard the sound of the box falling into the well and were happy.

That night they came to the well. The box was heavy and had landed deep down in the well. To get it, they would have to take out some of the water. They started drawing water from the well and pouring it onto the ground. Tony had made arrangements to make sure that the water reached his fruit trees. He had channels leading from the well to each of the trees.

By the time thieves found the box, they had drawn out enough water to water the trees. It was almost dawn. Tony sent for the soldiers, and just as the thieves were trying to open the box, they were caught red-handed.

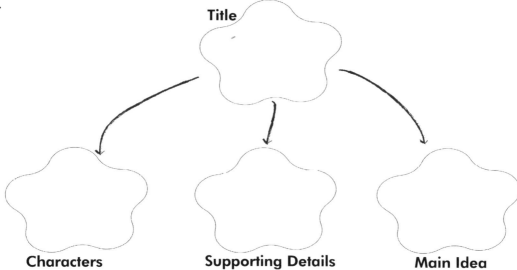

1. **Which details in the story show that Tony is really clever?**

    Ⓐ "Let us protect our valuables, and put all of our jewels in a box and throw them into the well. They will be safe there."
    Ⓑ He quickly told his son to put some large stones in a box and throw them into the well.
    Ⓒ Tony had made arrangements to make sure that the water reached the fruit trees. He had channels leading from the well to each of the trees.
    Ⓓ All of the above

Question 2-4 are based on the story below

After reading the story, enter the details in the map below. This will help you to answer the questions that follow.

The Glass Cupboard

There was a king who had a cupboard that was made entirely of glass. It was a special cupboard. It looked empty, but you could always take out anything you wanted. There was only one thing that had to be remembered. Whenever something was taken out of it, something else had to be put back in, although nobody knew why.

One day some thieves broke into the palace and stole the cupboard. "Now, we can have anything we want," they said. One of the thieves said, "I want a large bag of gold," and he opened the glass cupboard and got it. The other two did the same, and they, too, got exactly what they wanted. The thieves forgot one thing. Not one of them put anything back inside the cupboard.

This went on and on for weeks and months. At last, the leader of the thieves could bear it no longer. He took a hammer and smashed the glass cupboard into a million pieces, and then all three thieves fell down dead.

When the king returned home, he ordered his servants to search for the cupboard. When the servants found it and the dead thieves, they filled sixty great carts with the gold and took it back to the king. He said, "If those thieves had only put something back into the cupboard, they would be alive to this day."

He ordered his servants to collect all of the pieces of glass and melt into a globe of the world with all the countries on it; this was to remind himself and others, to give back something in return when someone shows an act of kindness or gives us something.

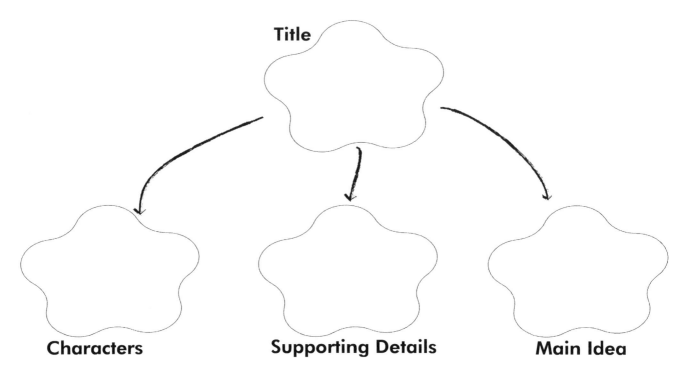

Characters   Supporting Details   Main Idea

2. Who are the main characters in the story?

   Ⓐ The king and his servants
   Ⓑ The king and the thieves
   Ⓒ The king's servants
   Ⓓ The glass cupboard thieves

3. How can the thieves best be described?

   Ⓐ Skillful and careful
   Ⓑ Greedy and careful
   Ⓒ Greedy and careless
   Ⓓ Unskilled and careful

4. The king in this story is _____.

   Ⓐ an ungrateful and rude person
   Ⓑ a dominating and greedy person
   Ⓒ a mean and selfish person
   Ⓓ a just and generous person

Question 5-8 are based on the story below

After reading the story, enter the details in the map below. This will help you to answer the questions that follow.

Do Your Best

Katie stood before the crowd, blushing and wringing her hands. She looked out and saw the room full of faces. Some she knew and some she did not. But, they were all here to listen to her. Taking a deep breath, she opened her mouth, but no words came out. Tears formed in the corners of her eyes as she closed them.

With her eyes closed, she imagined her mother helping her get dressed and ready for tonight. "Just do your best," is what her mother had told her. She opened her eyes and found her mother's smiling face in the crowd. Relaxing, she took another deep breath and started singing. She did not stop until she finished, and the crowd was on their feet applauding.

After the show, she found her parents and her friends. They all had wonderful things to say about her song and how proud they were because she kept going even when it seemed like she might give up. She shrugged her shoulders and shared a smile with her mother. "I just did my best," she answered.

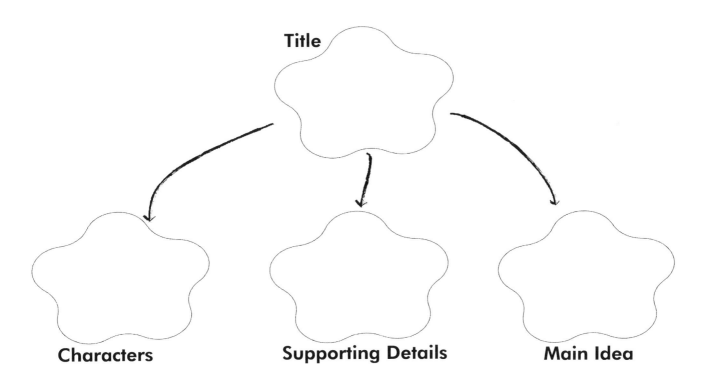

5. Who are the main characters in the above story?

   Ⓐ Katie, her mother, and her friends
   Ⓑ Katie and her mother
   Ⓒ Katie and her parents
   Ⓓ Katie and her friends

6. Who are the secondary characters is this story?

   Ⓐ Katie and her mother
   Ⓑ Katie's father and her mother
   Ⓒ Katie's father and her friends
   Ⓓ Katie and her friends

7. What does this story reveal about Katie's character?

   Ⓐ That she was a girl who gave up easily.
   Ⓑ That she was a girl who put forth effort to overcome her fears.
   Ⓒ That she had no talent at all.
   Ⓓ That she was meek and ran away from a difficult situation.

8. What does this story say about Katie's mother?

   Ⓐ She was very supportive.
   Ⓑ She was not supportive.
   Ⓒ She did not believe in singing.
   Ⓓ She wanted her daughter to make friends.

Question 9 and 10 are based on the story below

After reading the story, enter the details in the map below. This will help you to answer the questions that follow.

Late for School

Marrah heard the brakes on the bus as she shoveled the rest of her breakfast into her mouth. "You just missed the bus!" Marrah's mother yelled. "Why can't you ever be on time?"

"I'm sorry, Mom," Marrah sighed. She ran upstairs to her room so she could get her backpack, knowing she needed to hurry because her mother would have to take her to school.

"Let's go, Marrah!" Her mother called from downstairs. "You don't want to be late for school too!"

Frantic now, Marrah lifted her sheets to look under them before dropping to her knees in front of her bed. She pushed mounds of clothes out of the way as she continued to search for her backpack.

"Marrah!" Her mother called again, and she could hear the impatience in her mother's voice downstairs. She ran out of her room and leaned over the rail.

"I can't find my backpack!" She cried out.
"You mean this one?" Her mother pulled the bag from the floor beside her.
"Oh," she replied, her shoulders sagging as she walked down the stairs.

"Let's go to school, Marrah." Her mother said with a small smile on her face as they walked out the door.

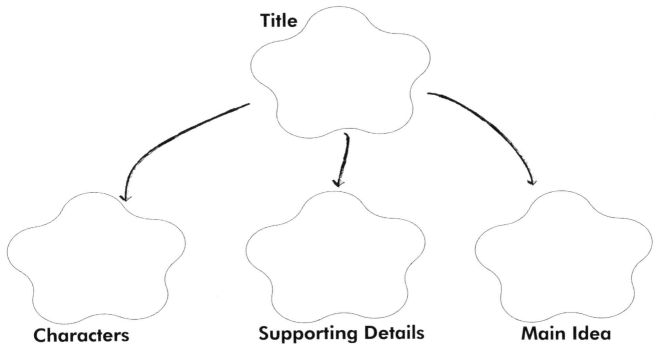

9. In the above story, Marrah appears to be _____ .

Ⓐ a very disorganized girl
Ⓑ a very organized girl
Ⓒ a very punctual girl
Ⓓ a very disciplined girl

10. What detail explains that Marrah's mother was kind even when she was frustrated with her daughter?

Ⓐ Her mother called again and she could hear the impatience in her voice downstairs.
Ⓑ "You just missed the bus!" Marrah's mother yelled. "Why can't you ever be on time?"
Ⓒ "Let's go, Marrah!" Her mother called from downstairs. "You don't want to be late to school too!"
Ⓓ "Let's go to school, Marrah." Her mother said with a small smile on her face as they walked out the door.

Question 11-13 are based on the story below

After reading the story, enter the details in the map below. This will help you to answer the questions that follow.

THE LITTLE PINK ROSE

Best Stories to Tell to Children (1912)
By Sara Cone Bryant

Once there was a little pink Rosebud, and she lived down in a little dark house under the ground.

One day she was sitting there, all by herself, and it was very still. Suddenly, she heard a little tap, tap, tap, at the door. "Who is that?" she said.

"It's the Rain, and I want to come in," said a soft, sad, little voice.

"No, you can't come in," the little Rosebud said. By and by she heard another little tap, tap, tap, on the windowpane. "Who is there?" she said.

The same soft, little voice answered, "It's the Rain, and I want to come in!"

"No, you can't come in," said the little Rosebud. Then she was very still for a long time. At last, there came a little rustling, whispering sound all around the window? rustle, whisper, whisper. "Who is there?" asked the little Rosebud.

"It's the Sunshine," said a little, soft, cheery voice, "and I want to come in!"

"N -- no," said the little pink rose, "you can't come in." And she sat still again.

Pretty soon, she heard the sweet little rustling noise at the key-hole. "Who is there?" she said.

"It's the Sunshine," said the cheery, little voice, "and I want to come in. I want to come in!"

"No, no," said the little pink rose, "you cannot come in."

By and by, as she sat so still, she heard tap, tap, tap and rustle, whisper, rustle all up and down the windowpane, and on the door, and at the key-hole. "Who is there?" she asked.

"It's the Rain and the Sunshine, the Rain and the Sunshine," said two little voices, together, "and we want to come in! We want to come in! We want to come in!"

"Dear, dear," said the little Rosebud, "if there are two of you, I s'pose I shall have to let you in." So she opened the door a little wee crack, and they came in. And one took one of her little hands, and the other took her other little hand, and they ran, ran, ran with her right up to the top of the ground. Then they said, --

"Poke your head through!"

So she poked her head through, and she was in the midst of a beautiful garden. It was springtime, and all the other flowers had their heads poked through, and she was the prettiest little pink rose in the whole garden!

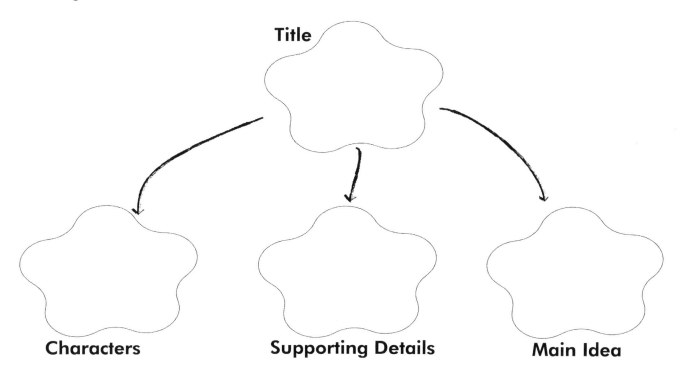

11. How can Rosebud best be described in the story?

Ⓐ She is excited and fearless.
Ⓑ She is happy and friendly.
Ⓒ She is shy and scared.
Ⓓ She is colorful and generous.

12. Part A
Who are the characters in the story?

Ⓐ Rosebud, Wind, Rain
Ⓑ Rosebud, Sun, Rain
Ⓒ Rosebud, Wind, Sun
Ⓓ Wind, Sun, Rain

Part B
Who are the secondary characters in the story?

Ⓐ Rosebud
Ⓑ Sun
Ⓒ Rain
Ⓓ Other flowers

13. How can Rosebud best be described in the story?

Do NOT write your answers in this book. To open the answer sheet, scan the QR code or visit *lumoslearning.com/a/5e005*

Chapter 1 → Lesson 5: Summarizing Texts

Question 1 is based on the story below

After reading the story, enter the details in the map below. This will help you to answer the questions that follow.

The Glass Cupboard

There was a king who had a cupboard that was made entirely of glass. It was a special cupboard. It looked empty, but you could always take out anything you wanted. There was only one thing that had to be remembered. Whenever something was taken out of it, something else had to be put back in, although nobody knew why.

One day some thieves broke into the palace and stole the cupboard. "Now, we can have anything we want," they said. One of the thieves said, "I want a large bag of gold," and he opened the glass cupboard and got it. The other two did the same, and they, too, got exactly what they wanted. The thieves forgot one thing. Not one of them put anything back inside the cupboard.

This went on and on for weeks and months. At last, the leader of the thieves could bear it no longer. He took a hammer and smashed the glass cupboard into a million pieces, and then all three thieves fell down dead.

When the king returned home, he ordered his servants to search for the cupboard. When the servants found it and the dead thieves, they filled sixty great carts with the gold and took it back to the king. He said, "If those thieves had only put something back into the cupboard, they would be alive to this day."

He ordered his servants to collect all of the pieces of glass and melt into a globe of the world with all the countries on it; this was to remind himself and others, to give back something in return when someone shows an act of kindness or gives us something.

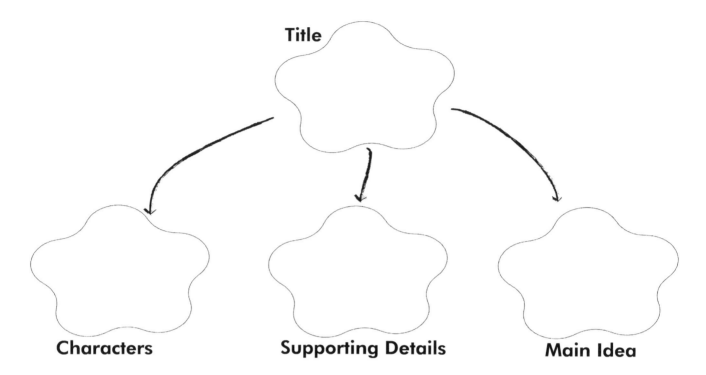

1. What is the passage about?

   Ⓐ It is about thieves getting greedy and breaking a glass cupboard.
   Ⓑ It is about a glass cupboard.
   Ⓒ It is about giving something back in return.
   Ⓓ All of the above

Question 2 is based on the story below

After reading the story, enter the details in the map below. This will help you to answer the questions that follow.

The Traveler

A weary traveler stopped at Sam's house and asked him for shelter for the night. Sam was a friendly soul. He not only agreed to let the traveler stay for the night; he decided to treat his guest to some curried chicken. So he bought a couple of chickens from the market and gave them to his wife to cook. Then he went off to buy some fruit.

Now, Sam's wife could not resist food. She had a habit of eating as she cooked. So as she cooked the meat, she smelled the rich steam and could not help tasting a piece. It was tender and delicious, and she decided to have another piece. Soon, there was only a tiny bit left. Her little son, Kevin, ran into the kitchen. She gave him that little piece.

Kevin found it so tasty that he begged his mother for more. But there was no more chicken left. The traveler, who had gone to have a wash, returned. The woman heard him coming and had to think of a plan quickly. She began to scold her son loudly: "Your father has taught you a shameful and disgusting habit. Stop it, I tell you!" The traveler was curious. "What habit has his father taught the child?" he asked. "Oh," said the woman, "Whenever a guest arrives, my husband cuts off their ears and roasts them for my son to eat."

The traveler was shocked. He picked up his shoes and fled.

"Why has our guest left in such a hurry?" asked Sam when he came back.

"A fine guest indeed!" exclaimed his wife. "He snatched the chickens out of my pot and ran off with them!"

"The chickens!" exclaimed Sam. He ran after his guest, shouting. "Let me have one, at least; you may keep the other!" But his guest only ran faster!

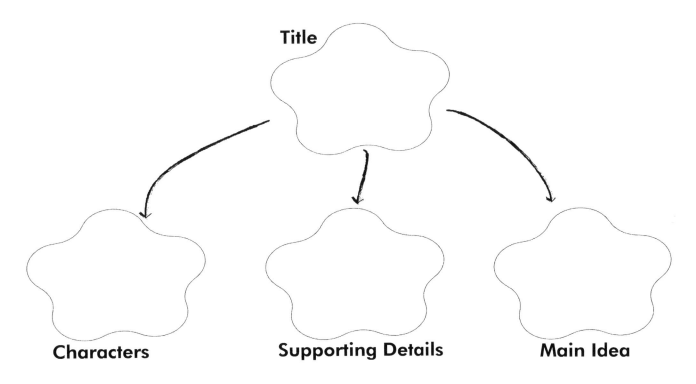

2. The above passage is about _____.

Ⓐ the wife who could not resist food and ate the chickens
Ⓑ the greedy traveler who ate all the chickens
Ⓒ Sam, who was a friendly soul
Ⓓ the son who ate the guest

Question 3 is based on the story below

A Clever Idea

Once, there was a severe drought. There was little water in Tony's well and he didn't know what would happen to the fruit trees in his garden. Just then, he noticed three men looking intently at his house. He was certain that the three were planning to rob his house.

He acted quickly. He shouted out to his son, "My son, because of the drought, money has become scarce. There are many thieves. Let us protect our valuables, and put all of our jewels in a box and throw them into the well. They will be safe there."

He quickly told his son to put some large stones in a box and throw them into the well. The thieves heard the sound of the box falling into the well and were happy.

That night they came to the well. The box was heavy and had landed deep down in the well. To get it, they would have to take out some of the water. They started drawing water from the well and pouring it onto the ground. Tony had made arrangements to make sure that the water reached his fruit trees. He had channels leading from the well to each of the trees.

By the time the thieves found the box, they had drawn out enough water to water the trees. It was almost dawn. Tony sent for the soldiers, and just as the thieves were trying to open the box, they were caught red-handed.

3. What is the above passage about?

Ⓐ It is about how the thieves watered the fruit garden.
Ⓑ It is about how clever Tony and his son tricked the thieves.
Ⓒ It is about how the thieves robbed Tony.
Ⓓ It is about two friends having fun being thieves.

Question 4 is based on the poem below

What is this life if, full of care,
We have no time to stand and stare?

No time to stand beneath the boughs
And stare as long as sheep or cows.

No time to see, when woods we pass,
Where squirrels hide their nuts in grass

No time to see, in broad daylight,
Streams full of stars, like skies at night.

No time to turn at Beauty's glance,
And watch her feet, how they can dance.

No time to wait till her mouth can
Enrich that smile her eyes began.

A poor life if, full of care,
We have no time to stand and stare.

- W. H. Davies

4. What is the poem about?

Ⓐ It is about life.
Ⓑ It is about how busy our lives are occasionally.
Ⓒ It is about the importance of taking time to do things that you like.
Ⓓ It is about life not being fair.

Question 5-8 are based on the story below

After reading the story, enter the details in the map below. This will help you to answer the questions that follow.

Do Your Best

Katie stood before the crowd, blushing and wringing her hands. She looked out and saw the room full of faces. Some she knew and some she did not. But, they were all here to listen to her. Taking a deep breath, she opened her mouth, but no words came out. Tears formed in the corners of her eyes as she closed them.

With her eyes closed, she imagined her mother helping her get dressed and ready for tonight. "Just do your best," is what her mother had told her. She opened her eyes and found her mother's smiling face in the crowd. Relaxing, she took another deep breath and started singing. She did not stop until she finished, and the crowd was on their feet applauding.

After the show, she found her parents and her friends. They all had wonderful things to say about her song and how proud they were because she kept going even when it seemed like she might give up. She shrugged her shoulders and shared a smile with her mother. "I just did my best," she answered.

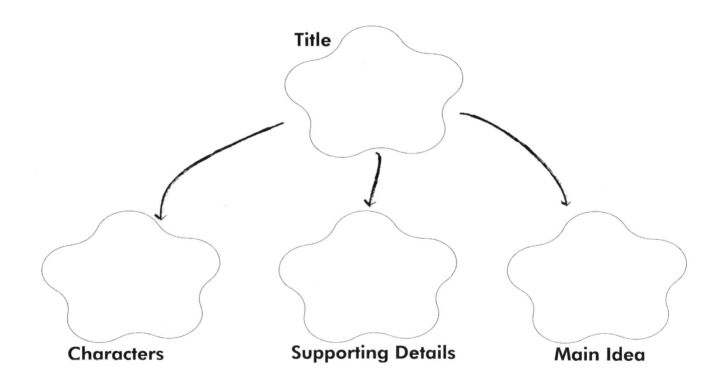

5. What is this story about?

   Ⓐ Never give up when you have friends.
   Ⓑ Believe in yourself and you can do your best.
   Ⓒ Listen to your friends.
   Ⓓ Give up when you are nervous.

6. What does the first paragraph tell the reader?

   Ⓐ Katie is nervous about the beginning of the movie.
   Ⓑ Katie is nervous about performing.
   Ⓒ Katie is nervous about her new dress.
   Ⓓ Katie is not nervous anymore because she remembered her mother's words.

7. The second paragraph of the story tells the importance of _____.

   Ⓐ taking a deep breath
   Ⓑ a mother's love
   Ⓒ encouragement that kindles self confidence
   Ⓓ a smiling face

8. In the third paragraph, Katie's parents and friends _____.

   Ⓐ criticize her for being nervous at the beginning
   Ⓑ applaud her for her singing talent
   Ⓒ are proud of her because she kept going even though she was nervous
   Ⓓ both 'b' and 'c'

Question 9 and 10 are based on the story below

After reading the story, enter the details in the map below. This will help you to answer the questions that follow.

Late for School

Marrah heard the air in the bus brakes as she shoveled the rest of her breakfast into her mouth. "You just missed the bus!" Marrah's mother yelled. "Why can't you ever be on time?"

"I'm sorry, Mom," Marrah sighed. She ran upstairs to her room so she could get her backpack, knowing she needed to hurry because her mother would have to take her to school.

"Let's go, Marrah!" Her mother called from downstairs. "You don't want to be late to school too!"

Frantic now, Marrah lifted her sheets to look under them before dropping to her knees in front of her bed. She pushed mounds of clothes out of the way as she continued to search for her backpack,

"Marrah!" Her mother called again, and she could hear the impatience in her voice downstairs. She ran out of her room and leaned over the rail.

"I can't find my backpack!" She cried out.
"You mean this one?" Her mother pulled the bag from the floor beside her.
"Oh," she replied, her shoulders sagging as she walked down the stairs.

"Let's go to school, Marrah." Her mother said with a small smile on her face as they walked out the door.

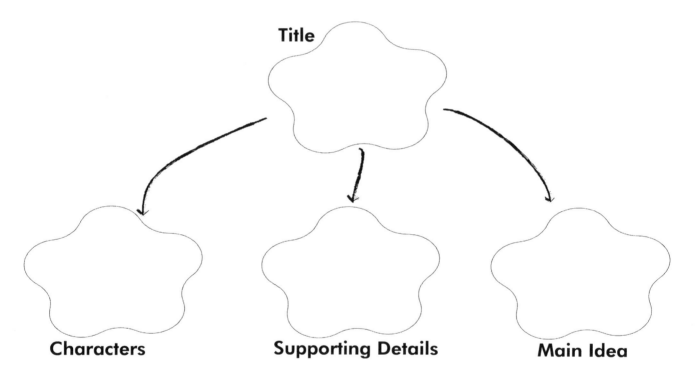

9. What is this story about?

Ⓐ It is about the importance of being on-time to school.
Ⓑ It is about an argument between Marrah and her mother.
Ⓒ It is about what can happen when you are not organized.
Ⓓ It is about the importance of being disorganized.

10. What does the fifth paragraph tell the reader?

Ⓐ Marrah's room is clean and organized.
Ⓑ Marrah's mother is impatient.
Ⓒ Marrah is ready for school.
Ⓓ Marrah's room is messy and disorganized.

Question 11 is based on the story below

After reading the story, enter the details in the map below. This will help you to answer the questions that follow.

THE LITTLE PINK ROSE

Best Stories to Tell to Children (1912)
By Sara Cone Bryant

Once there was a little pink Rosebud, and she lived down in a little dark house under the ground. One day she was sitting there, all by herself, and it was very still. Suddenly, she heard a little tap, tap, tap, at the door. "Who is that?" she said.

"It's the Rain, and I want to come in," said a soft, sad, little voice.

"No, you can't come in," the little Rosebud said. By and by she heard another little tap, tap, tap, on the windowpane. "Who is there?" she said.

The same soft, little voice answered, "It's the Rain, and I want to come in!"

"No, you can't come in," said the little Rosebud. Then she was very still for a long time. At last, there came a little rustling, whispering sound all around the window? rustle, whisper, whisper. "Who is there?" asked the little Rosebud.

"It's the Sunshine," said a little, soft, cheery voice, "and I want to come in!"

"N -- no," said the little pink rose, "you can't come in." And she sat still again.

Pretty soon, she heard the sweet little rustling noise at the key-hole. "Who is there?" she said.

"It's the Sunshine," said the cheery, little voice, "and I want to come in. I want to come in!"

"No, no," said the little pink rose, "you cannot come in."

By and by, as she sat so still, she heard tap, tap, tap and rustle, whisper, rustle all up and down the windowpane, and on the door, and at the key-hole. "Who is there?" she asked.

"It's the Rain and the Sunshine, the Rain and the Sunshine," said two little voices, together, "and we want to come in! We want to come in! We want to come in!"

"Dear, dear," said the little Rosebud, "if there are two of you, I s'pose I shall have to let you in." So she opened the door a little wee crack, and they came in. And one took one of her little hands, and the other took her other little hand, and they ran, ran, ran with her right up to the top of the ground. Then they said, --
"Poke your head through!"

So she poked her head through, and she was in the midst of a beautiful garden. It was springtime, and all the other flowers had their heads poked through, and she was the prettiest little pink rose in the whole garden!

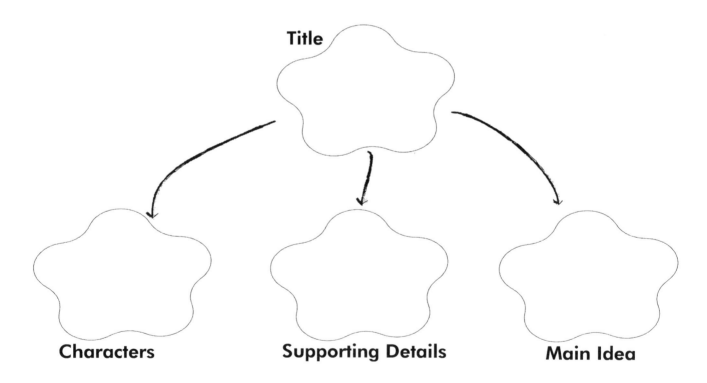

11 Part A
What is this story about?

Ⓐ Taking the time to do things we like
Ⓑ Good things happen when you take a risk.
Ⓒ Flowers in a garden.
Ⓓ The importance of the sun and the rain.

Part B
What happened in the bold section at the end of the story?

Ⓐ Rosebud hid in the garden.
Ⓑ Rosebud hid in her house.
Ⓒ Rosebud made new friends with Sun and Rain.
Ⓓ Rosebud bloomed into a beautiful rose.

Question 12 is based on the paragraph below

My mother works extremely hard as a nurse. Each day she gives her all, and when she comes home, she is dog tired. I like to help her take a load off, so I try and make dinner for her. I also clean the house and mow the yard outside. Today was even more difficult, though. It rained like cats and dogs all afternoon, so I couldn't take care of the yard. Then, when I came inside to clean, I realized the kitchen sink was clogged, and the washing machine seemed broken. I couldn't catch a break! By the time Mom came home, I had given up, called a plumber, and ordered a pizza. It's a good thing my mom always taught me that where there is a will, there is a way!

12. Why does the author want to help his mother?

Ⓐ She is gone all day.
Ⓑ She works hard as a nurse.
Ⓒ She does not like housework.
Ⓓ She is a new mother.

Question 13 is based on the passage below

My cousin lives in California. Because that is such a long distance from Philadelphia, it is not a short drive, so I only see her once a year. This distance makes it so hard to visit her, and I miss her very much.

Our parents think it is too hard to drive across the country to see each other. I want to see her more often so we can see movies together, but our parents say no!

13. What is this passage about?

Ⓐ The author wants to see his/her cousin.
Ⓑ The author's parents do not like to drive.
Ⓒ The author's cousin does not like to see movies.
Ⓓ The author wants to move to California.

Question 14 is based on the paragraph below

The American colonists have to formulate a plan to declare independence from Great Britain. Although the reasons vary, at the core, they want independence because they believe Great Britain takes away the rights of the colonists. But, without any real specificity of those reasons, other countries will have a difficult time supporting this new nation, and they must accumulate support if they are going to be able to break away.

14. What is this passage about?

Ⓐ The importance of the colonists formulating a plan.
Ⓑ The importance of the colonists having other countries help them.
Ⓒ The importance of the colonists fighting Great Britain.
Ⓓ The importance of disliking Great Britain.

Do NOT write your answers in this book. To open the answer sheet, scan the QR code or visit **lumoslearning.com/a/5e006**

Chapter 1 → Lesson 6: Events

Question 1 is based on the story below

After reading the story, enter the details in the map below. This will help you to answer the questions that follow.

Salmon

A fish that is a great favorite with people is salmon. It begins its life in a small pool up a river. Far from the sea, the fish lays its eggs in a pool in the river. When the baby fish are a few inches long, they begin to swim down the river. As they grow bigger, they make their way towards the sea.

They jump over rocks, often with their tails first. Suddenly, they find themselves in the sea. The fish live in the sea for three years. They swim far away from land. How do they find their way back? These fish have a wonderful sense of smell. They remember the scent of their journey easily because the river flowed to the sea and carried them there. After three years, most salmon swim toward the pools.

As soon as they reach a pool, the females lay their eggs. They lay their eggs near the edge of the water and cover them with sand. Soon the eggs hatch, and the pool is full of small fish, getting ready for the long journey out to the sea.

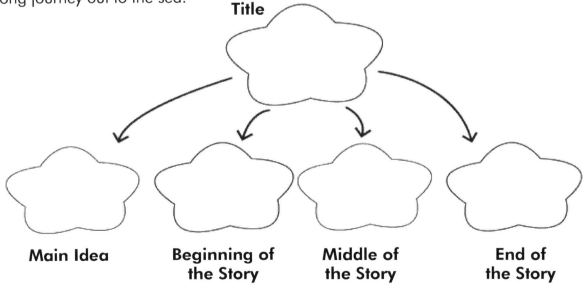

1. What is the first important event that happens in this story?

   Ⓐ Salmon are a favorite of many people.
   Ⓑ The fish lay their eggs in the river.
   Ⓒ The fish live in the ocean for three years.
   Ⓓ The fish swim to the ocean.

Question 2-4 are based on the story below

After reading the story, enter the details in the map below. This will help you to answer the questions that follow.

A Clever Idea

Once, there was a severe drought. There was little water in Tony's well and he didn't know what would happen to the fruit trees in his garden. Just then, he noticed three men looking intently at his house. He was certain that the three were planning to rob his house. He acted quickly. He shouted out to his son, "My son, due to the drought, money has become scarce. There are many thieves. Let us protect our valuables, and put all of our jewels in a box and throw them into the well. They will be safe there." He quickly told his son to put some large stones in a box and throw them into the well.

The thieves heard the sound of the box falling into the well and were happy. That night they came to the well. The box was heavy and had landed deep down in the well. To get it, they would have to take out some of the water. They started drawing water from the well and pouring it onto the ground. Tony had made arrangements to make sure that the water reached his fruit trees. He had channels leading from the well to each of the trees. By the time thieves found the box, they had drawn out enough water to water the trees. It was almost dawn. Tony sent for the soldiers, and just as the thieves were trying to open the box, they were caught red-handed.

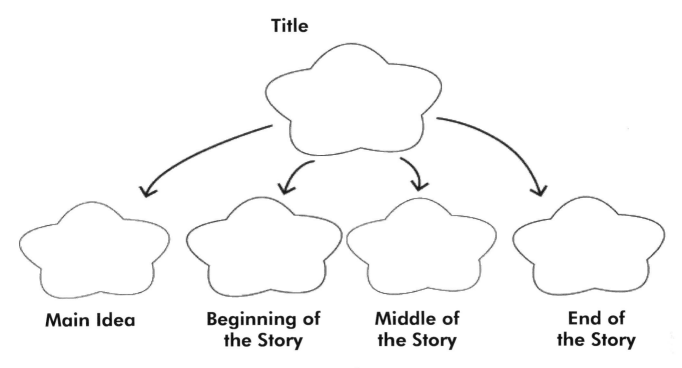

| Main Idea | Beginning of the Story | Middle of the Story | End of the Story |

2. **Which sentence shows the correct timeline of events?**

   Ⓐ Tony could not water his fields; Tony told his son to throw their valuable possessions down the well; The thieves get the box from the well; Tony's fields are watered.
   Ⓑ Tony told his son to throw their valuable possessions down the well; Tony could not water his fields; The thieves get the box from the well; Tony's fields are watered.
   Ⓒ Tony's fields are watered; Tony told his son to throw their valuable possessions down the well; Tony could not water his fields; The thieves get the box from the well.
   Ⓓ The thieves get the box from the well; Tony's fields are watered; Tony told his son to throw their valuable possessions down the well; Tony could not water his fields.

3. **What led to little water being in Tony's well?**

   Ⓐ thieves
   Ⓑ a severe drought
   Ⓒ watering fruit trees
   Ⓓ none of the above

4. **What happened at the end?**

   Ⓐ The well was full of water.
   Ⓑ The thieves were caught.
   Ⓒ The trees were not watered.
   Ⓓ Tony hid the valuables.

Question 5 is based on the story below

After reading the story, enter the details in the map below. This will help you to answer the questions that follow.

Do Your Best

Katie stood before the crowd, blushing and wringing her hands. She looked out and saw the room full of faces. Some she knew and some she did not. But, they were all here to listen to her. Taking a deep breath, she opened her mouth, but no words came out. Tears formed in the corners of her eyes as she closed them.

With her eyes closed, she imagined her mother helping her get dressed and ready for tonight. "Just do your best," is what her mother had told her. She opened her eyes and found her mother's smiling face in the crowd. Relaxing, she took another deep breath and started singing. She did not stop until she finished, and the crowd was on their feet applauding.

After the show, she found her parents and her friends. They all had wonderful things to say about her song and how proud they were because she kept going even when it seemed like she might give up. She shrugged her shoulders and shared a smile with her mother. "I just did my best," she answered.

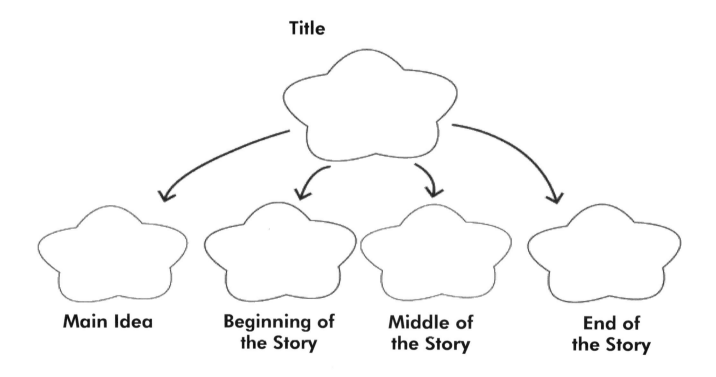

5. **What happened the second time Katie took a deep breath?**

   Ⓐ She looked at her mother.
   Ⓑ She could not sing.
   Ⓒ She sang beautifully.
   Ⓓ She cried.

6. **Using the letter at the beginning of each sentence, put the sentences into the correct order to make a paragraph.**

   A. Emily asks her mother to put the pan in the oven.
   B. Emily loves to cook.
   C. Emily loves brownies.
   D. Emily asks her mother if she can make a snack.
   E. She mixes the brownie mix, eggs, and oil together and pours them in a pan.

   Ⓐ B, C, D, E, A
   Ⓑ B, D, C, E, A
   Ⓒ A, B, D, E, C
   Ⓓ E, C, A, D, B

Question 7 and 8 are based on the story below

After reading the story, enter the details in the map below. This will help you to answer the questions that follow.

Late for School

Marrah heard the brakes on the bus as she shoveled the rest of her breakfast into her mouth. "You just missed the bus!" Marrah's mother yelled. "Why can't you ever be on time?"

"I'm sorry, Mom," Marrah sighed. She ran upstairs to her room so she could get her backpack, knowing she needed to hurry because her mother would have to take her to school.

"Let's go, Marrah!" Her mother called from downstairs. "You don't want to be late for school too!"

Frantic now, Marrah lifted her sheets to look under them before dropping to her knees in front of her bed. She pushed mounds of clothes out of the way as she continued to search for her backpack.

"Marrah!" Her mother called again, and she could hear the impatience in her mother's voice downstairs. She ran out of her room and leaned over the rail.

"I can't find my backpack!" She cried out.

"You mean this one?" Her mother pulled the bag from the floor beside her.

"Oh," she replied, her shoulders sagging as she walked down the stairs.

"Let's go to school, Marrah." Her mother said with a small smile on her face as they walked out the door.

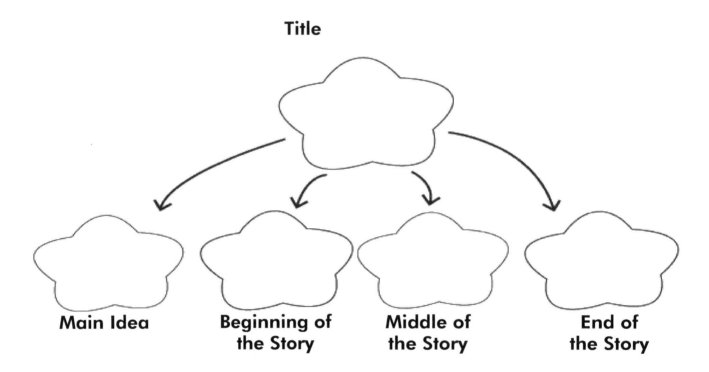

7. Which major event occurred first in the story?

   Ⓐ The school bus arrived.
   Ⓑ Marrah finished her breakfast.
   Ⓒ Marrah searched for her bag.
   Ⓓ Marrah ran down the stairs.

8. Which major event occurred at the end of the story?

   Ⓐ Her mother took Marrah to school because she missed her school bus.
   Ⓑ Marrah was still searching for her backpack.
   Ⓒ Marrah took a day off from school.
   Ⓓ Marrah's school bus waited for her to take her to school.

9. Using the letter at the beginning of each sentence, put the sentences below into the correct order to make a paragraph.

A. Janie plays with her puppy.
B. Janie realizes her puppy is covered with mud.
C. Janie grabs the shampoo and water hose.
D. She changes into play clothes.
E. Janie washes and dries her puppy.

- Ⓐ E, C, D, B, A
- Ⓑ B, D, C, E, A
- Ⓒ C, B, A, D, E
- Ⓓ A, C, E, D, B

10. What does Emily do after she gets her mother's permission to make a snack?

A. Emily asks her mother to put the pan in the oven.
B. Emily loves to cook.
C. Emily loves her brownies.
D. Emily asks her mother if she can make a snack.
E. She mixes the brownie mix, eggs, and oil together and pours them in a pan.

- Ⓐ Emily asks her mother to put the pan in the oven.
- Ⓑ Emily asks her mother if she can make a snack.
- Ⓒ She mixes the brownie mix, eggs, and oil together and pours them in a pan.
- Ⓓ None of the above

11. All the below events took place because _____.

A. Emily asks her mother to put the pan in the oven.
B. Emily loves to cook.
C. Emily loves her brownies.
D. Emily asks her mother if she can make a snack.
E. She mixes the brownie mix, eggs, and oil together and pours them in a pan.

- Ⓐ Emily loves her brownies.
- Ⓑ Emily loves to cook.
- Ⓒ Emily's mother puts the pan in the oven.
- Ⓓ Emily wanted a snack.

Question 12-14 are based on the story below

After reading the story, enter the details in the map below. This will help you to answer the questions that follow.

THE LITTLE PINK ROSE

Best Stories to Tell to Children (1912)
By Sara Cone Bryant

Once there was a little pink Rosebud, and she lived down in a little dark house under the ground. One day she was sitting there, all by herself, and it was very still. Suddenly, she heard a little tap, tap, tap, at the door. "Who is that?" she said.

"It's the Rain, and I want to come in," said a soft, sad, little voice.

"No, you can't come in," the little Rosebud said. By and by she heard another little tap, tap, tap, on the windowpane. "Who is there?" she said.

The same soft little, voice answered, "It's the Rain, and I want to come in!"

"No, you can't come in," said the little Rosebud. Then she was very still for a long time. At last, there came a little rustling, whispering sound all around the window? rustle, whisper, whisper. "Who is there?" asked the little Rosebud.

"It's the Sunshine," said a little, soft, cheery voice, "and I want to come in!"

"N -- no," said the little pink rose, "you can't come in." And she sat still again.

Pretty soon, she heard the sweet little rustling noise at the key-hole. "Who is there?" she said.

"It's the Sunshine," said the cheery, little voice, "and I want to come in. I want to come in!"

"No, no," said the little pink rose, "you cannot come in."

By and by, as she sat so still, she heard tap, tap, tap and rustle, whisper, rustle all up and down the windowpane, and on the door, and at the key-hole. "Who is there?" she asked.

"It's the Rain and the Sunshine, the Rain and the Sunshine," said two little voices, together, "and we want to come in! We want to come in! We want to come in!"

"Dear, dear," said the little Rosebud, "if there are two of you, I s'pose I shall have to let you in." So she opened the door a little wee crack, and they came in. And one took one of her little hands, and the other took her other little hand, and they ran, ran, ran with her right up to the top of the ground.

Then they said, --

"Poke your head through!"

So she poked her head through, and she was in the midst of a beautiful garden. It was springtime, and all the other flowers had their heads poked through, and she was the prettiest little pink rose in the whole garden!

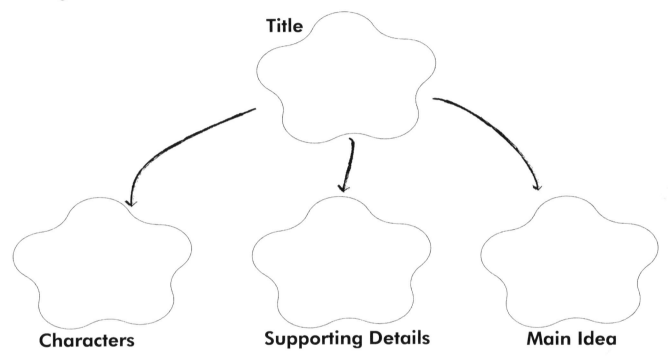

12. **Sequence the events in the proper order so that they form the correct timeline of the story. Enter your answers in correct sequence in the boxes given below**

   A. Rosebud poked her head above ground.
   B. Rosebud heard a strange sound
   C. Rosebud let her visitors in;
   D. Rosebud had visitors;

   1.
   2.
   3.
   4.

13. Which event happened first in the story?

Ⓐ Little Rosebud heard a tap, tap, tap.
Ⓑ Little Rosebud had visitors.
Ⓒ Little Rosebud refused to open her door.
Ⓓ Little Rosebud stuck her head above ground.

14. How would the last event be different if Rosebud never let her visitors in?

Ⓐ She would meet the Sun.
Ⓑ She would meet the Rain.
Ⓒ She would not bloom.
Ⓓ She would not be quiet.

Do NOT write your answers in this book. To open the answer sheet, scan the QR code or visit **lumoslearning.com/a/5e007**

Chapter 1 → Lesson 7: Setting

Question 1 and 2 are based on the story below

After reading the story, enter the details in the map below. This will help you to answer the questions that follow.

A Clever Idea

Once there was a severe drought. There was little water in Tony's well, and he didn't know what would happen to the fruit trees in his garden. Just then, he noticed three men looking intently at his house. He was certain that the three strangers were planning to rob his house. He acted quickly. He shouted out to his son, "My son, due to the drought, money has become scarce. There are many thieves. Let us protect our valuables, and put all of our jewels in a box and throw them into the well. They will be safe there." He quickly told his son to put some large stones in a box and throw them into the well.

The thieves heard the sound of the box falling into the well and were happy. That night they came to the well. The box was heavy and had landed deep down in the well. To get it, they would have to take out some of the water. They started drawing water from the well and pouring it onto the ground. Tony had made arrangements to make sure that the water reached his fruit trees. He had channels leading from the well to each of the trees. By the time thieves found the box, they had drawn out enough water to water the trees. It was almost dawn. Tony sent for the soldiers, and just as the thieves were trying to open the box, they were caught red-handed.

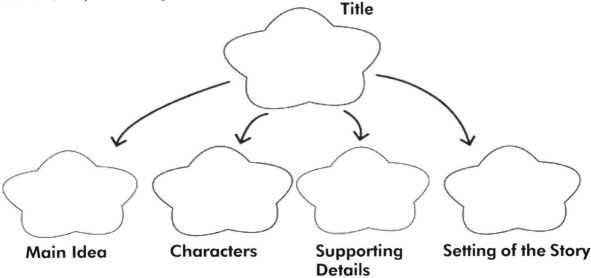

LumosLearning.com

1. **What is the setting of the story?**

   Ⓐ It takes place in the countryside.
   Ⓑ It takes place in Tony's backyard.
   Ⓒ Both A and B
   Ⓓ None of the above

2. **Which detail in the above story tells us that this story possibly took place during the past?**

   Ⓐ "Tony sent for the soldiers, and just as the thieves were trying to open the box, they were caught red-handed."
   Ⓑ "Once there was a severe drought."
   Ⓒ He shouted out to his son, "My son, due to the drought, money has become scarce."
   Ⓓ "By the time the thieves found the box, they had drawn out enough water to water the trees."

Question 3 and 4 are based on the story below

After reading the story, enter the details in the map below. This will help you to answer the questions that follow.

Do Your Best

Katie stood before the crowd, blushing and wringing her hands. She looked out and saw the room full of faces. Some she knew and some she did not. But, they were all here to listen to her. Taking a deep breath, she opened her mouth, but no words came out. Tears formed in the corners of her eyes as she closed them.

With her eyes closed, she imagined her mother helping her get dressed and ready for tonight. "Just do your best," is what her mother had told her. She opened her eyes and found her mother's smiling face in the crowd. Relaxing, she took another deep breath and started singing. She did not stop until she finished, and the crowd was on their feet applauding.

After the show, she found her parents and her friends. They all had wonderful things to say about her song and how proud they were because she kept going even when it seemed like she might give up. She shrugged her shoulders and shared a smile with her mother. "I just did my best," she answered.

3. **Where does this story take place?**

   Ⓐ It takes place in Katie's backyard.
   Ⓑ It takes place at the local pool.
   Ⓒ It takes place in an auditorium.
   Ⓓ None of the above

4. Which sentence indicates that Katie had to sing in front of a lot of people?

Ⓐ She did not stop until she finished and the crowd was on their feet applauding.
Ⓑ Katie stood before the crowd blushing and wringing her hands.
Ⓒ She looked out and saw the room full of faces.
Ⓓ All of the above

Question 5 is based on the story below

After reading the story, enter the details in the map below. This will help you to answer the questions that follow.

Late for School

Marrah heard the brakes on the bus as she shoveled the rest of her breakfast into her mouth. "You just missed the bus!" Marrah's mother yelled. "Why can't you ever be on time?"

"I'm sorry, Mom," Marrah sighed. She ran upstairs to her room so she could get her backpack, knowing she needed to hurry because her mother would have to take her to school.

"Let's go, Marrah!" Her mother called from downstairs. "You don't want to be late for school too!"

Frantic now, Marrah lifted her sheets to look under them before dropping to her knees in front of her bed. She pushed mounds of clothes out of the way as she continued to search for her backpack.

"Marrah!" Her mother called again, and she could hear the impatience in her mother's voice downstairs. She ran out of her room and leaned over the rail.

"I can't find my backpack!" She cried out.

"You mean this one?" Her mother pulled the bag from the floor beside her.

"Oh," she replied, her shoulders sagging as she walked down the stairs.

"Let's go to school, Marrah." Her mother said with a small smile on her face as they walked out the door.

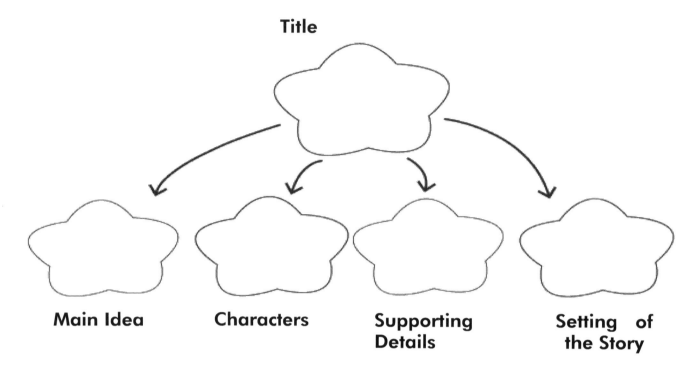

5. What is the setting of this story?

   Ⓐ It takes place at Marrah's house.
   Ⓑ It takes place at Marrah's school.
   Ⓒ It takes place on Marrah's bus.
   Ⓓ It takes place in Marrah's backyard.

Question 6 is based on the story below

After reading the story, enter the details in the map below. This will help you to answer the questions that follow.

Once there was a severe drought. There was little water in Tony's well, and he didn't know what would happen to the fruit trees in his garden. Just then, he noticed three men looking intently at his house.

He was certain that the three strangers were planning to rob his house. He acted quickly. He shouted out to his son, "My son, due to the drought, money has become scarce. There are many thieves.

Let us protect our valuables, and put all of our jewels in a box and throw them into the well. They will be safe there." He quickly told his son to put some large stones in a box and throw them into the well.

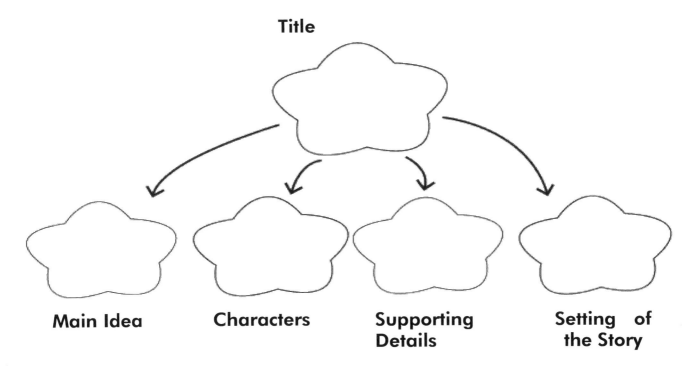

6. The author uses the phrase "a severe drought" to show that this story is set in a time when _____.

  Ⓐ there is too much rain.
  Ⓑ there is too much light.
  Ⓒ there is not enough light.
  Ⓓ there is not enough rain.

Question 7 is based on the poem below

In the kitchen,
After the aimless
Chatter of the plates,
The murmur of the stoves,
The chuckles of the water pipes,
And the sharp exchanges
Of the knives, forks and spoons,
Comes the serious quiet
When the sink slowly clears its throat,
And you can hear the occasional rumble
Of the refrigerator's tummy
As it digests the cold.

7. What is the setting of this poem?

Ⓐ It is set in a house.
Ⓑ It is set in the stove.
Ⓒ It is set in a restaurant.
Ⓓ It is set in a kitchen.

8. What is likely the setting for the story she is reading?

Sally is reading a story about two wounded soldiers, their capture, and their escape from the enemy's camp.

Ⓐ a cinema theatre
Ⓑ a school auditorium
Ⓒ a battlefield
Ⓓ a circus

9. The setting of this story is _____.

Mike is reading a story about spaceships, satellites, space stations, and invading aliens. There were wars in the sky, and astronauts were trying to save their spaceship. The astronauts won the war against some aliens who wanted to rule earth.

Ⓐ on earth
Ⓑ in outer space
Ⓒ in the ocean
Ⓓ none of the above

10. Select the phrase that best completes the sentence below.

Setting is important, because it tells the audience _____.

Ⓐ where and what the story is about
Ⓑ where and how the story is told
Ⓒ where and when the story takes place
Ⓓ who tells the story

Question 11 is based on the story below

After reading the story, enter the details in the map below. This will help you to answer the questions that follow.

THE LITTLE PINK ROSE

Best Stories to Tell to Children (1912)
By Sara Cone Bryant

Once there was a little pink Rosebud, and she lived down in a little dark house under the ground. One day she was sitting there, all by herself, and it was very still. Suddenly, she heard a little tap, tap, tap, at the door. "Who is that?" she said.

"It's the Rain, and I want to come in," said a soft, sad, little voice.

"No, you can't come in," the little Rosebud said. By and by she heard another little tap, tap, tap, on the windowpane. "Who is there?" she said.

The same soft little voice answered, "It's the Rain, and I want to come in!"

"No, you can't come in," said the little Rosebud. Then it was very still for a long time. At last, there came a little rustling, whispering sound, all around the window: rustle, whisper, whisper. "Who is there?" said the little Rosebud.

"It's the Sunshine," said a little, soft, cheery voice, "and I want to come in!"

"N -- no," said the little pink rose, "you can't come in." And she sat still again.

Pretty soon, she heard the sweet little rustling noise at the key-hole. "Who is there?" she said.

"It's the Sunshine," said the cheery little voice, "and I want to come in. I want to come in!"

"No, no," said the little pink rose, "you cannot come in."

By and by, as she sat so still, she heard tap, tap, tap, and rustle, whisper, rustle, all up and down the windowpane, and on the door, and at the key-hole. "Who is there?" she said.

"It's the Rain and the Sun, the Rain and the Sun," said two little voices, together, "and we want to come in! We want to come in! We want to come in!"

"Dear, dear," said the little Rosebud, "if there are two of you, I s'pose I shall have to let you in." So she opened the door a little wee crack, and they came in. And one took one of her little hands, and the other took her other little hand, and they ran, ran, ran with her, right up to the top of the ground. Then they said, --
"Poke your head through!"

So she poked her head through, and she was in the midst of a beautiful garden. It was springtime, and all the other flowers had their heads poked through, and she was the prettiest little pink rose in the whole garden!

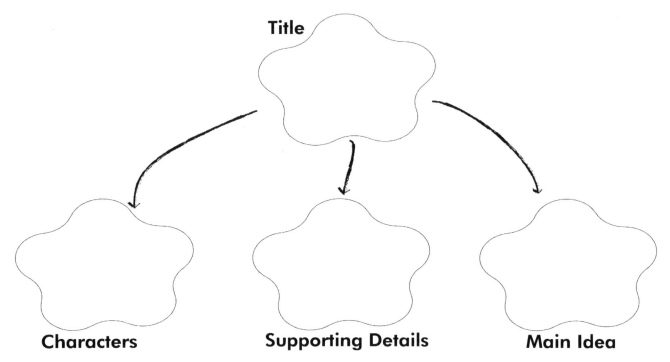

11. **Part A**
    What is the main setting of the above story?

    Ⓐ In a garden
    Ⓑ In a forest
    Ⓒ In a town
    Ⓓ In a zoo

Part B
Which sentence indicates that the majority of the story takes place below ground?

Ⓐ So she opened the door a little wee crack, and they came in.
Ⓑ She was the prettiest little pink rose in the whole garden!
Ⓒ By and by, as she sat so still, she heard tap, tap, tap, and rustle, whisper, rustle, all up and down the windowpane, and on the door, and at the key-hole.
Ⓓ And one took one of her little hands, and the other took her other little hand, and they ran, ran, ran with her, right up to the top of the ground.

12. If a setting is important to the story, it is usually established _____.

   Ⓐ at the end
   Ⓑ at the beginning
   Ⓒ in the middle
   Ⓓ only by illustrations

13. Setting can be established through _____.

   Ⓐ mood and description
   Ⓑ character traits
   Ⓒ dialogue
   Ⓓ all of the above

14. Setting is rarely important in _____.

   Ⓐ stories that are fairy tales
   Ⓑ descriptions of battle
   Ⓒ descriptions of a wealthy home
   Ⓓ stories set in outer space

Do NOT write your answers in this book. To open the answer sheet, scan the QR code or visit **lumoslearning.com/a/5e008**

Chapter 1 → Lesson 8: Figurative Language

1. **Select the phrase that best completes the sentence.**

   A simile is _____.

   Ⓐ a figure of speech that compares two things.
   Ⓑ a figure of speech that compares two things using the words 'like' or 'as'.
   Ⓒ a figure of speech that describes an image.
   Ⓓ a figure of speech that gives an object human characteristics.

   Question 2 is based on the paragraph below

Under the snow-white coverlet, upon a snow-white pillow, lay the most beautiful girl that Tom had ever seen. Her cheeks were very white, and her hair was like threads of gold spread all over her pillow.

2. **Select the phrase that best completes the sentence.**

   The second sentence is an example of _____.

   Ⓐ a metaphor
   Ⓑ personification
   Ⓒ a detailed sentence
   Ⓓ a simile

Question 3-5 are based on the poem below

My daddy is a tiger
My mother is a bear
My sister is a pest
Who messes with my hair
And even though my home
Is like living in a zoo
I know my family loves me
And will take care of me too

3. How many similes are in the poem above?

- Ⓐ One
- Ⓑ Two
- Ⓒ Three
- Ⓓ Four

4. How many metaphors are in the poem?

- Ⓐ One
- Ⓑ Two
- Ⓒ Three
- Ⓓ Four

5. An example of a simile in this poem would be _____.

- Ⓐ my mother is a bear
- Ⓑ my father is a tiger
- Ⓒ my sister is a pest
- Ⓓ my home is like living in a zoo

6. What two objects does the simile below compare?

A cloud floats like a feather in the sky.

- Ⓐ It compares a cloud and the sky.
- Ⓑ It compares a cloud and a feather.
- Ⓒ It compares a feather and the sky.
- Ⓓ It compares the sky with nothing.

LumosLearning.com

7. Which of the following is another appropriate simile for the sentence below?

  Ⓐ A cloud floats like a rock in the water.
  Ⓑ A cloud floats like a bird in the sky.
  Ⓒ A cloud floats like a leaf in the wind.
  Ⓓ A cloud floats like a cotton ball in a jar.

Question 8 is based on the details below

My daddy is a tiger
My mother is a bear
My sister is a pest
Who messes with my hair

8. What would be another similar metaphor for the author's sister?

  Ⓐ My sister is a bug.
  Ⓑ My sister is like a pest.
  Ⓒ My sister is annoying.
  Ⓓ My sister is like a bug.

9. The expression, 'he is a cat' is _____.

  The trapeze artist in the circus was amazing. He leaped effortlessly through the air and landed on his feet so smoothly. All I can say is that he is a cat!

  Ⓐ a metaphor
  Ⓑ a simile
  Ⓒ an idiom
  Ⓓ a proverb

10. The expression, once in a blue moon, is an example of _____.

  My mother is very particular about giving me healthy food. I only eat French fries once in a blue moon.

  Ⓐ an idiom
  Ⓑ a simile
  Ⓒ a metaphor
  Ⓓ none of the above

11. Read each sentence and match it to the correct figure of speech

	a simile	personification	metaphor
The sea glittered like diamonds under the harsh sun rays.	○	○	○
The spoon ran away to find a better home.	○	○	○
The pillow was as soft as cotton.	○	○	○
The biscuit was a paper weight.	○	○	○

Do NOT write your answers in this book. To open the answer sheet, scan the QR code or visit **lumoslearning.com/a/5e009**

Chapter 1 → Lesson 9: Structure of Text

Question 1 is based on the story below

After reading the story, enter the details in the map below. This will help you to answer the questions that follow.

The Orange

Even though no one knows exactly where oranges come from, Southeast Asia is believed to be their first home. They are grown today in most of the warmer parts of the world. The ancient Greeks and Romans knew about oranges. It is possible that oranges were carried from India to Western Asia and then to Europe.

The Spaniards took the sour oranges to the West Indies and from there to Florida, in America. Today, oranges are the most important fresh fruit in international trade. There are three different kinds of oranges: the sweet or common orange, the mandarin orange, and the sour or bitter orange.

One type of sweet orange is called the blood orange. It has a pulp with a deep red color. This type of orange is grown mostly in the Mediterranean region. Mandarin oranges are mainly found in Florida. Sour oranges are grown almost everywhere, with Spain having the greatest number used for trade. These sour oranges are generally used to make marmalade.

However, they can be put to many other interesting uses, from making medicine to creating perfumes. Oranges have many medicinal values. Oranges are the fruit with the greatest concentration of vitamin C. The skin of the orange helps to keep the fruit inside from becoming damaged and to remain clean. The thick, oily, and bitter skin does not allow any insects to get into an orange. Many kinds of useful oils can be extracted from the thick skin. Oranges are healthy and delicious.

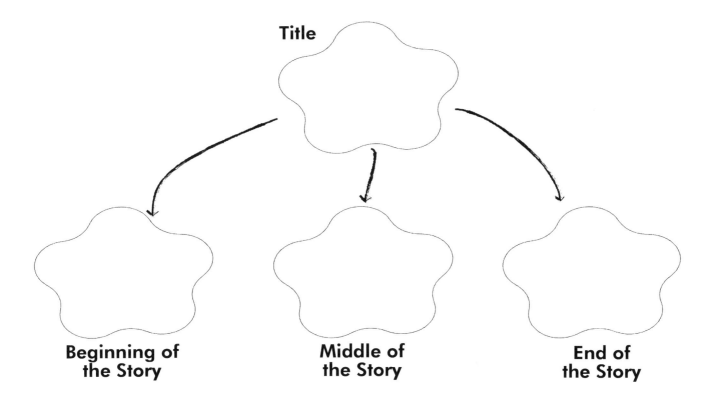

1. Where can you find the conclusion of this passage?

   Ⓐ At the beginning of the passage.
   Ⓑ In the middle of the passage.
   Ⓒ At the end of the passage.
   Ⓓ A passage never has an ending.

Question 2 and 3 are based on the poem below

What is this life if, full of care,
We have no time to stand and stare?

No time to stand beneath the boughs
And stare as long as sheep or cows.

No time to see, when woods we pass,
Where squirrels hide their nuts in grass

No time to see, in broad daylight,
Streams full of stars, like skies at night.

No time to turn at Beauty's glance,
And watch her feet, how they can dance.

No time to wait till her mouth can
Enrich that smile her eyes began.'

A poor life if, full of care,
We have no time to stand and stare

-- W. H. Davies

2. What is the first stanza of the poem doing?

Ⓐ Asking a question.
Ⓑ Answering a question.
Ⓒ Introducing life.
Ⓓ Introducing the poet.

3. Who wrote this poem?

Ⓐ An unknown poet
Ⓑ W. H. Davies
Ⓒ Robert Browning
Ⓓ William Wordsworth

4. When you read a humorous piece of writing, you usually _____.

   Ⓐ cry
   Ⓑ become serious
   Ⓒ write down information
   Ⓓ laugh

5. A passage that is an example of descriptive writing _____.

   Ⓐ is a letter written to a person
   Ⓑ creates a clear and vivid picture of a person, place, or thing
   Ⓒ describes an experience in a personal voice
   Ⓓ is a dialogue between two people

6. In a poem, we often find _____.

   Ⓐ rhyming words
   Ⓑ rhythmic writing
   Ⓒ dialogues
   Ⓓ 'a' and 'b'

7. Which of the following is not a genre of fiction?

   Ⓐ poetry
   Ⓑ mystery
   Ⓒ fairy tale
   Ⓓ informational

8. Which of the following is not a genre of nonfiction?

   Ⓐ newspaper article
   Ⓑ mystery
   Ⓒ biography
   Ⓓ informational

Question 9 is based on the poem below

In the kitchen,
After the aimless

Chatter of the plates,
The murmur of the stoves,

The chuckles of the water pipes,
And the sharp exchanges

Of the knives, forks, and spoons,
Comes the serious quiet

When the sink slowly clears its throat,
And you can hear the occasional rumble

Of the refrigerator's tummy
As it digests the cold.

9. The above lines are a _____.

Ⓐ story
Ⓑ poem
Ⓒ passage
Ⓓ song

Question 10 and 11 are based on the story below

After reading the story, enter the details in the map below. This will help you to answer the questions that follow.

Once there was a severe drought. There was little water in Tony's well, and he didn't know what would happen to the fruit trees in his garden. Just then, he noticed three men looking intently at his house. He was certain that the three strangers were planning to rob his house. He acted quickly. He shouted out to his son, "My son, due to the drought, money has become scarce. There are many thieves. Let us protect our valuables, and put all of our jewels in a box and throw them into the well. They will be safe there." He quickly told his son to put some large stones in a box and throw them into the well. The thieves heard the sound of the box falling into the well and were happy.

That night they came to the well. The box was heavy and had landed deep down in the well. To get it, they would have to take out some of the water. They started drawing water from the well and pouring it onto the ground. Tony had made arrangements to make sure that the water reached his fruit trees. He had channels leading from the well to each of the trees.

By the time thieves found the box, they had drawn out enough water to water the trees. It was almost dawn. Tony sent for the soldiers, and just as the thieves were trying to open the box, they were caught red-handed.

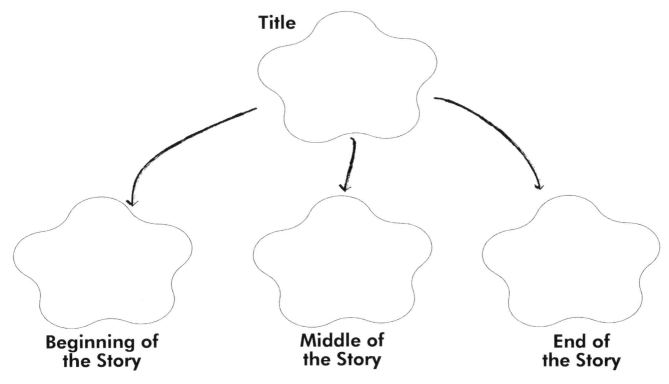

10. What is one of the main things that the above story is missing?

Ⓐ It is missing the introduction to the story.
Ⓑ It is missing the conclusion to the story.
Ⓒ It is missing the title of the story.
Ⓓ It is missing the description of the characters.

11. We have been studying the aftermath of volcanoes. I have a lot of information, but I cannot write a research report.
What type of text structure could best be used to explain the research fictionally?

Ⓐ Create a short story
Ⓑ Create a cause and effect essay
Ⓒ Create a visual illustration
Ⓓ Create a diary

Do NOT write your answers in this book. To open the answer sheet, scan the QR code or visit **lumoslearning.com/a/5e010**

Chapter 1 → Lesson 10: Styles of Narration

Question 1 is based on the story below

After reading the story, enter the details in the map below. This will help you to answer the questions that follow.

Late for School

Marrah heard the brakes on the bus as she shoveled the rest of her breakfast into her mouth. "You just missed the bus!" Marrah's mother yelled. "Why can't you ever be on time?"

"I'm sorry, Mom," Marrah sighed. She ran upstairs to her room so she could get her backpack, knowing she needed to hurry because her mother would have to take her to school.

"Let's go, Marrah!" Her mother called from downstairs. "You don't want to be late for school too!"

Frantic now, Marrah lifted her sheets to look under them before dropping to her knees in front of her bed. She pushed mounds of clothes out of the way as she continued to search for her backpack.

"Marrah!" Her mother called again, and she could hear the impatience in her mother's voice downstairs. She ran out of her room and leaned over the rail.

"I can't find my backpack!" She cried out.
"You mean this one?" Her mother pulled the bag from the floor beside her.
"Oh," she replied, her shoulders sagging as she walked down the stairs.

"Let's go to school, Marrah." Her mother said with a small smile on her face as they walked out the door.

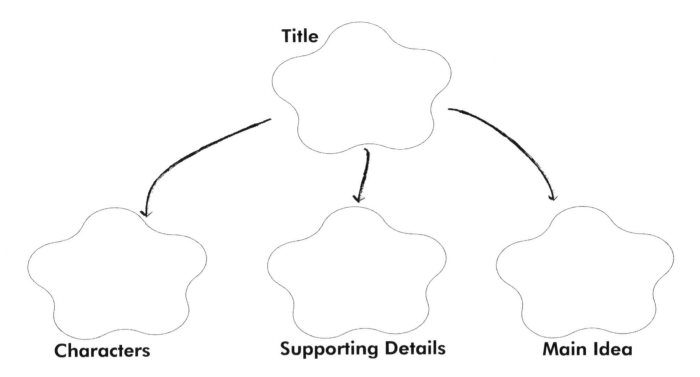

1. How might this story be different if the author told it from the point of view of Marrah's mother?

   Ⓐ The story would have described Marrah's frustration.
   Ⓑ The story would not change.
   Ⓒ The story would describe her mother's frustration.
   Ⓓ The story would focus on the bus driver's experience.

2. Select the phrase that best completes the below sentence.

   The first person point of view _____.

   Ⓐ has the character tell the story in his own words and uses the word "I".
   Ⓑ has the character tell the story in his own words and uses pronouns like "he" and "she."
   Ⓒ has the ability to show what is happening in many places but does not reveal the thoughts of the characters.
   Ⓓ has the narrator tell the story to another character using the pronoun "you."

3. Select the phrase that best completes the below sentence.

The second person point of view _____.

Ⓐ has the character tell the story in his own words and uses the pronoun "I."
Ⓑ has the character tell the story in his own words and uses pronouns like "he" and "she."
Ⓒ has the ability to show what is happening in many places but cannot see the thoughts of the characters.
Ⓓ has the narrator tell the story to the reader using the pronoun "you."

4. Which sentence is written in the first person point of view?

Ⓐ Kelsey walked to school today.
Ⓑ She walked to school today.
Ⓒ I walked to school today.
Ⓓ The neighbor walks to school every day.

5. Which sentence is written in the third person point of view?

Ⓐ I just won the race!
Ⓑ Did you think the race was really long?
Ⓒ She won the race.
Ⓓ none of the above

6. Why is it important for the author to keep the same point of view throughout the whole text?

Ⓐ It makes writing the story easy.
Ⓑ It makes the characters fun.
Ⓒ It makes the reader think about the message of the story.
Ⓓ It keeps the story clear and easier to understand.

7. Select the phrase that best completes the sentence below.

Narrative writing is the style of writing which_____.

Ⓐ describes an experience in a personal voice
Ⓑ is written in verse and is rhythmic
Ⓒ is a fairy tale
Ⓓ none of the above

8. Which point of view is typically found in a diary or journal?

   Ⓐ omniscient
   Ⓑ first
   Ⓒ second
   Ⓓ third

9. If a piece of writing deals with the solution of a crime or the unraveling of secrets, it is called a _____.

   Ⓐ an autobiography
   Ⓑ a biography
   Ⓒ mystery
   Ⓓ a fairy tale

10. What point of view is the following sentence in?

    Kelsey was extremely upset. While she and Danny were together, he got lost.

    Ⓐ omniscient
    Ⓑ first
    Ⓒ second
    Ⓓ third

Question 11 is based on the story below

After reading the story, enter the details in the map below. This will help you to answer the questions that follow.

THE LITTLE PINK ROSE

Best Stories to Tell to Children (1912)
By Sara Cone Bryant

Once there was a little pink Rosebud, and she lived down in a little dark house under the ground. One day she was sitting there, all by herself, and it was very still. Suddenly, she heard a little tap, tap, tap, at the door. "Who is that?" she said.

"It's the Rain, and I want to come in," said a soft, sad, little voice.

"No, you can't come in," the little Rosebud said. By and by she heard another little tap, tap, tap, on the windowpane. "Who is there?" she said.

The same soft, little voice answered, "It's the Rain, and I want to come in!"

"No, you can't come in," said the little Rosebud. Then she was very still for a long time. At last, there came a little rustling, whispering sound all around the window? rustle, whisper, whisper. "Who is there?" said the little Rosebud.

"It's the Sunshine," said a little, soft, cheery voice, "and I want to come in!"

"N -- no," said the little pink rose, "you can't come in." And she sat still again.

Pretty soon, she heard the sweet little rustling noise at the key-hole. "Who is there?" she said.

"It's the Sunshine," said the cheery, little voice, "and I want to come in. I want to come in!"

"No, no," said the little pink rose, "you cannot come in."

By and by, as she sat so still, she heard tap, tap, tap and rustle, whisper, rustle all up and down the windowpane, and on the door, and at the key-hole. "Who is there?" she asked.

"It's the Rain and the Sunshine, the Rain and the Sunshine," said two little voices, together, "and we want to come in! We want to come in! We want to come in!"

"Dear, dear," said the little Rosebud, "if there are two of you, I s'pose I shall have to let you in." So she opened the door a little wee crack, and they came in. And one took one of her little hands, and the other took her other little hand, and they ran, ran, ran with her right up to the top of the ground.

Then they said, --

"Poke your head through!"

So she poked her head through, and she was in the midst of a beautiful garden. It was springtime, and all the other flowers had their heads poked through, and she was the prettiest little pink rose in the whole garden!

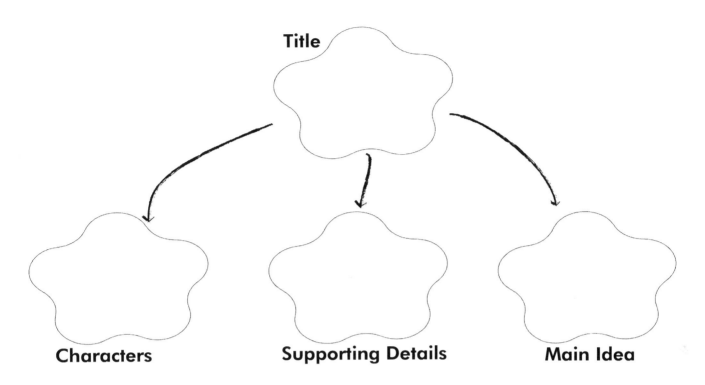

11. How might this story be different if it were told from the point of view of the sun?

12. Read each sentence and match it to the point of view from which it is being told

	First Person	Third Person
While we were walking together, I lost my dog.	○	○
Kelsey was extremely upset. While she and Danny were together, he got lost.	○	○
This is the first time we have had a chance to go to the zoo.	○	○

Do NOT write your answers in this book. To open the answer sheet, scan the QR code or visit **lumoslearning.com/a/5e011**

Chapter 1 → Lesson 11: Visual Elements

Question 1 and 2 are based on the passage below

Eliza stood beside the winding train. It seemed to go on for miles and miles! The noise was unbearable at times, and she was constantly dirty. Ma and Pa told her that this would not be a fun way to travel, but she was so excited to go that she said she did not care. Now, all that Eliza can think of is a clean bed and a quiet rest.

1. **Select the phrase that best completes the below sentence.**

   Without the added image, the reader might _____.

   Ⓐ think Eliza is describing a car ride.
   Ⓑ think Eliza is describing an actual train ride.
   Ⓒ believe the author is confused.
   Ⓓ think the author needs more details.

2. **What is media in relation to text?**

   Ⓐ Media uses sounds, images, and language.
   Ⓑ Media uses sounds, movies, and language.
   Ⓒ Media uses sounds, verbs, and metaphors.
   Ⓓ Media uses sounds, similes, and alliteration.

3. **Select the phrase that best completes the below sentence.**

   Charts, graphs, pictures, and maps are examples of _____.

   Ⓐ images of text
   Ⓑ visual elements of text
   Ⓒ needless attachments to text
   Ⓓ none of the above

4. **How does a timeline enhance text as a visual element?**

   Ⓐ It provides factual information.
   Ⓑ It provides the key events mentioned in the text in the order that they occurred.
   Ⓒ It provides illustrations.
   Ⓓ It provides location information of places mentioned in the text.

5. **Please select the phrase that best completes the below sentence.**

   The above illustration is titled "The Nutcracker".

   Without looking at the image in detail, the reader might assume from only reading the title, that the image is about _____.

   Ⓐ a song about nuts
   Ⓑ a commercial about a company selling nuts
   Ⓒ a story about a squirrel named "The Nutcracker"
   Ⓓ an article on the health benefits of nuts

6. **How does a map enhance text as a visual element?**

   Ⓐ It provides factual information.
   Ⓑ It provides the key events mentioned in the text in the order that they occurred.
   Ⓒ It provides key information as illustrations.
   Ⓓ It provides the location information of places mentioned in the text.

7. **Some examples of facts that are presented in visual form are _____.**

   Ⓐ graphs
   Ⓑ charts
   Ⓒ essays
   Ⓓ both 'a' and 'b'

8. **Select the phrase that best completes the sentence.**

   Some common types of graphs that present data are _____ .

   Ⓐ bar graphs
   Ⓑ line graphs
   Ⓒ pie graphs
   Ⓓ all of the above

9. **Select the option that best completes the sentence.**

   A graph is a _____ that shows the relationship between changing things.

   Ⓐ movie
   Ⓑ circular
   Ⓒ chart or drawing
   Ⓓ all the above

10. **Which visual aid works best in fictional text?**

    Ⓐ an internet link
    Ⓑ illustration
    Ⓒ text only
    Ⓓ bar graph

Question 11 and 12 are based on the details below

Tommy cannot decide what sort of top he should wear. Closing his eyes, he imagines all of the different ones he has.

11. **Select the phrase that best completes the below sentence.**

    The picture adds additional information to the text because it _____.

    Ⓐ helps visual learners.
    Ⓑ defines the top as a shirt that he would like to wear.
    Ⓒ does not add any information.
    Ⓓ defines the top as a type of hat.

12. **Select the phrase that best completes the below sentence.**

    Without the added image, the reader might assume _____.

    Ⓐ that Tommy is talking about shirts.
    Ⓑ that the author is confused.
    Ⓒ that Tommy is confused.
    Ⓓ that Tommy is playing a game.

13. **Which visual aid works best in informational text?**

    Ⓐ Internet link
    Ⓑ illustration
    Ⓒ text only
    Ⓓ bar graph

Do NOT write your answers in this book. To open the answer sheet, scan the QR code or visit **lumoslearning.com/a/5e012**

Chapter 1 → Lesson 12: Compare and Contrast

Question 1 is based on the stories below

Late for School

Marrah heard the brakes on the bus as she shoveled the rest of her breakfast into her mouth. "You just missed the bus!" Marrah's mother yelled. "Why can't you ever be on time?"

"I'm sorry, Mom," Marrah sighed. She ran upstairs to her room so she could get her backpack, knowing she needed to hurry because her mother would have to take her to school.

"Let's go, Marrah!" Her mother called from downstairs. "You don't want to be late for school too!" Frantic now, Marrah lifted her sheets to look under them before dropping to her knees in front of her bed. She pushed mounds of clothes out of the way as she continued to search for her backpack.

"Marrah!" Her mother called again, and she could hear the impatience in her mother's voice downstairs. She ran out of her room and leaned over the rail.

"I can't find my backpack!" She cried out.
"You mean this one?" Her mother pulled the bag from the floor beside her.
"Oh," she replied, her shoulders sagging as she walked down the stairs.
"Let's go to school, Marrah." Her mother said with a small smile on her face as they walked out the door.

Do Your Best

Katie stood before the crowd, blushing and wringing her hands. She looked out and saw the room full of faces. Some she knew and some she did not. But, they were all here to listen to her. Taking a deep breath, she opened her mouth, but no words came out. Tears formed in the corners of her eyes as she closed them.

With her eyes closed, she imagined her mother helping her get dressed and ready for tonight. "Just do your best," is what her mother had told her. She opened her eyes and found her mother's smiling face in the crowd. Relaxing, she took another deep breath and started singing. She did not stop until she finished, and the crowd was on their feet applauding.

After the show, she found her parents and her friends. They all had wonderful things to say about her song and how proud they were because she kept going even when it seemed like she might give up. She shrugged her shoulders and shared a smile with her mother. "I just did my best," she answered.

1. How are Katie and Marrah similar?

Ⓐ Both girls have dark hair.
Ⓑ Both girls are the same age.
Ⓒ Both girls rely on their mothers.
Ⓓ Both girls have many friends.

Question 2 is based on the poems below

What is this life if, full of care,
We have no time to stand and stare?

No time to stand beneath the boughs
And stare as long as sheep or cows.

No time to see, when woods we pass,
Where squirrels hide their nuts in grass

No time to see, in broad daylight,
Streams full of stars, like skies at night.

No time to turn at Beauty's glance,
And watch her feet, how they can dance.

No time to wait till her mouth can
Enrich that smile her eyes began.

A poor life if, full of care,
We have no time to stand and stare.

-- W. H. Davies

In the kitchen,
After the aimless
Chatter of the plates,
The murmur of the stoves,
The chuckles of the water pipes,
And the sharp exchanges

Of the knives, forks, and spoons,
Comes the serious quiet
When the sink slowly clears its throat,
And you can hear the occasional rumble
Of the refrigerator's tummy
As it digests the cold.

2. How are these two poems similar?

Ⓐ Both poems use similes.
Ⓑ Both poems use personification.
Ⓒ Both poems use colorful descriptions.
Ⓓ Both poems use metaphors.

3. What things might you look for when comparing two pieces of text?

Ⓐ type of text
Ⓑ purpose of text
Ⓒ style of text
Ⓓ all of the above

4. When using a Venn diagram to compare and contrast two characters, what does the overlapping section of the circles show?

Ⓐ It describes the traits the characters have in common.
Ⓑ It describes the traits the characters do not have in common.
Ⓒ It describes all the characteristics of both characters.
Ⓓ It does not do any of the above.

5. When using a Venn diagram to compare and contrast two characters, what do the outer, non-overlapping parts of the circles represent?

Ⓐ They describe the traits the characters have in common.
Ⓑ They describe the traits the characters do not have in common.
Ⓒ Be all the characteristics of both characters.
Ⓓ They do not do any of the above.

6. From the below table, which two months had the largest number of library books borrowed?

Number of library books borrowed in 2016	
Month	Number of books borrowed
September	660
October	670
November	570
December	475

- Ⓐ September and December
- Ⓑ September and October
- Ⓒ October and November
- Ⓓ October and December

7. Refer to the chart above to complete the sentence below.

Students borrowed the least number of books in _____ 2016.

- Ⓐ November
- Ⓑ October
- Ⓒ September
- Ⓓ December

8. Pick the sentence that compares the above sets of words correctly.

    a. Math, Science, Social Studies, History
    b. Basketball, Soccer, Baseball, Tennis

- Ⓐ Choice 'a' contains subjects related to cognitive activity whereas 'b' contains games that are related to physical activity.
- Ⓑ Choice 'a' contains subjects that we study whereas 'b' contains the games that we play.
- Ⓒ Choice 'a' contains subjects that are easy whereas 'b' contains games that are difficult to play.
- Ⓓ Both 'a' and 'b' are correct.

9. Which sentence would lead you to compare two items?

- Ⓐ Presidents Lincoln and Kennedy had several similarities during their terms in office.
- Ⓑ The American Revolution and the Civil War had many differences.
- Ⓒ The two pets could not be more diverse from each other.
- Ⓓ How are tornados different from hurricanes?

10. Which sentence would lead you to contrast two items?

- Ⓐ My brother is exactly like my father.
- Ⓑ How are tornados similar to hurricanes?
- Ⓒ How is my mother's cake unlike my grandmother's?
- Ⓓ How are tornadoes similar to tsunamis?

11. Which sentence would lead you to compare two items?

- Ⓐ What is the difference between Marrah and her mother?
- Ⓑ How is my mother's cake similar to my grandmother's?
- Ⓒ The two pets could not be more different from each other.
- Ⓓ How are tornados different from hurricanes?

12. Which sentence would lead you to compare two items?

- Ⓐ My brother is exactly like my father.
- Ⓑ What is the difference between Marrah and her mother?
- Ⓒ The two pets could not be more different from each other.
- Ⓓ How are tornados different from hurricanes?

13. Which sentence would lead you to contrast two items?

- Ⓐ My brother is exactly like my father.
- Ⓑ What is the difference between Marrah and her mother?
- Ⓒ How is my mother's cake similar to my grandmother's?
- Ⓓ How are tornados similar to hurricanes?

14. Which sentence would lead you to contrast two items?

- Ⓐ My brother is exactly like my father.
- Ⓑ How are tornados similar to hurricanes?
- Ⓒ How is my mother's cake similar to my grandmother's?
- Ⓓ How are tornados different from hurricanes?

15. Explain what the words in the following set have in common?

   Lincoln, Washington, Kennedy, Clinton

   Ⓐ They are all names of airports in the United States of America
   Ⓑ They are all names of former America's presidents.
   Ⓒ They are names of some states in the United States of America.
   Ⓓ None of the above

End of Reading Literature

Chapter 2
Reading Informational Text

Do NOT write your answers in this book. To open the answer sheet, scan the QR code or visit **lumoslearning.com/a/5e013**

Lesson 1: Inferences and Conclusions

Question 1 and 2 are based on the paragraph below

It was a cool, crisp morning. Lucy threw her backpack over her shoulders, jumped on her bicycle, and pedaled down Pine Street. Her tires made soft crunching noises as she drove through piles of brown, yellow, and orange leaves.

1. In the paragraph above, what time of year do you think it was?

    Ⓐ Fall
    Ⓑ Spring
    Ⓒ Summer
    Ⓓ Winter

2. Where do you think Lucy is going?

    Ⓐ to her home
    Ⓑ to visit friends
    Ⓒ to school
    Ⓓ to the supermarket

Question 3 and 4 are based on the paragraph below

Mrs. Davis lived in a great big apartment on the top floor of her building. As the doctor walked into her spacious, clean apartment, he noticed fine, leather furniture and expensive works of art. Mrs. Davis sat up in her large, king-sized bed wearing a beautiful, silk robe. Dr. Thomas took Mrs. Davis's temperature and listened to her heart. "You seem to be feeling better this afternoon, Mrs. Davis," commented the doctor.

3. What can you infer about Mrs. Davis after reading the passage above?

   Ⓐ Mrs. Davis is a wealthy woman.
   Ⓑ Mrs. Davis is an intelligent woman.
   Ⓒ Mrs. Davis is a beautiful woman.
   Ⓓ Mrs. Davis is a young woman.

4. After reading the paragraph above, what can you infer about the reason for Dr. Thomas's visit?

   Ⓐ Dr. Thomas is visiting Mrs. Davis because she was sick.
   Ⓑ Dr. Thomas is visiting Mrs. Davis because he is her new neighbor.
   Ⓒ Dr. Thomas is visiting Mrs. Davis because he needs a favor.
   Ⓓ Dr. Thomas is visiting Mrs. Davis because it is her birthday.

5. Based on the sentence below, draw a conclusion about the way that Jan feels about the creature.

   Jan took one look at the hideous creature and ran away as fast as she could.

   Ⓐ She thinks the creature is cute.
   Ⓑ She thinks the creature is scary.
   Ⓒ She feels sorry for the creature.
   Ⓓ None of the above

6. Select the phrase that best completes the sentence.

   Kara's mother wakes up at 5:30 A.M. every morning so she'll have time to study for her college classes. This is the only time she has to study before she has to go to work. She takes college classes two nights a week. Every weekend, she volunteers at the local homeless shelter. She has been helping out there for the past three years.

   From the information in the paragraph above, one can infer that Kara's mother is probably _____.

   Ⓐ married to a college professor
   Ⓑ a very hard-working woman
   Ⓒ tired of going to college
   Ⓓ None of the above

7. Select the phrase that best complete the sentence.

Victor took off his reading glasses and rubbed his eyes. He picked up his walking cane. Then he slowly used the cane to help himself up from the bench. Every day, it takes him a little bit longer to stand up. Every day, it becomes more difficult for him to walk.

From the information in the paragraph above, you can infer that Victor is _____.

Ⓐ a young man
Ⓑ happy
Ⓒ an old man
Ⓓ in good health

8. Select the phrase that best completes the sentence.

You can infer from the paragraph that _____.

Ⓐ Victor was reading before he decided to stand up.
Ⓑ It is difficult for Victor to get up from the bench.
Ⓒ Victor doesn't walk very well.
Ⓓ All of the above.

9. What conclusion can you draw about Corky from the sentences below?

Corky waddled toward the lake. When he reached the water, he flapped his wings, quacked, and jumped in.

Ⓐ Corky is a dog.
Ⓑ Corky is a duck.
Ⓒ Corky is a fish.
Ⓓ Corky is a horse.

10. What do you think "read between the lines" means?

Authors help readers make inferences by giving certain details. However, authors expect readers to "read between the lines."

Ⓐ Figure out what text means.
Ⓑ Look for evidence in text to make inferences.
Ⓒ Come up with ideas or opinions of your own based on what you read.
Ⓓ All of the above

Do NOT write your answers in this book. To open the answer sheet, scan the QR code or visit **lumoslearning.com/a/5e014**

Chapter 2 → Lesson 2: The Main Idea and Supporting Details

Question 1-5 are based on the passage below

After reading the passage, enter the details in the map below. This will help you to answer the questions that follow.

The Orange

Even though no one knows exactly where oranges come from, Southeast Asia is believed to be their first home. They are grown today in most of the warmer parts of the world. The ancient Greeks and Romans knew about oranges. It is possible that oranges were carried from India to Western Asia and then to Europe.

The Spaniards took the sour oranges to the West Indies and from there to Florida, in America. Today, oranges are the most important fresh fruit in international trade. There are three different kinds of oranges: the sweet or common orange, the mandarin orange, and the sour or bitter orange.

One type of sweet orange is called the blood orange. It has a pulp with a deep red color. This type of orange is grown mostly in the Mediterranean region. Mandarin oranges are mainly found in Florida. Sour oranges are grown almost everywhere, with Spain having the greatest number used for trade. These sour oranges are generally used to make marmalade.

However, they can be put to many other interesting uses, from making medicine to creating perfumes. Oranges have many medicinal values. Oranges are the fruit with the greatest concentration of vitamin C. The skin of the orange helps to keep the fruit inside from becoming damaged and to remain clean. The thick, oily, and bitter skin does not allow any insects to get into an orange. Many kinds of useful oils can be extracted from the thick skin. Oranges are healthy and delicious.

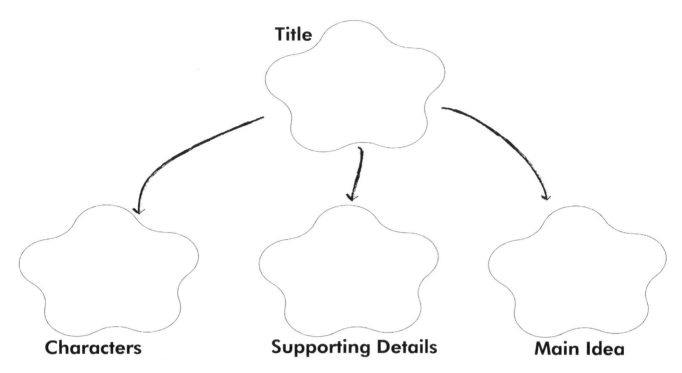

1. What is the author saying about oranges in the first paragraph?

    Ⓐ The author is explaining how oranges have been dispersed around the world.
    Ⓑ The author is explaining how the ancient Romans and Greeks knew about oranges.
    Ⓒ The author is explaining how oranges are traded around the world.
    Ⓓ None of the above

2. From your understanding of the above passage, oranges are grown in ___.

    Ⓐ Spain
    Ⓑ the West Indies
    Ⓒ most of the colder parts of the word.
    Ⓓ most of the warmer parts of the world.

3. Where in the passage can you find out about who grows the sour oranges and where they are grown?

    Ⓐ The second paragraph
    Ⓑ The third paragraph
    Ⓒ Both A and B.
    Ⓓ In the last paragraph

4. Which detail in the above passage supports the fact that the orange is a clean fruit?

Ⓐ Anyone touching it only touches the outer covering, which is easily taken off.
Ⓑ The thick, oily, and bitter skin does not allow insects to get into the orange.
Ⓒ Both A and B
Ⓓ None, because the orange is a very messy fruit.

5. The second paragraph tells us _____ .

Ⓐ about the types of oranges
Ⓑ about where the oranges are grown
Ⓒ about the usefulness of oranges
Ⓓ All of the above

Question 6 and 7 are based on the passage below

After reading the passage, enter the details in the map below. This will help you to answer the questions that follow.

Salmon

A fish that is a great favorite with people is salmon. It begins its life in a small pool up a river. Far from the sea, the fish lays its eggs in a pool in the river. When the baby fish are a few inches long, they begin to swim down the river. As they grow bigger, they make their way towards the sea.

They jump over rocks, often with their tails first. Suddenly, they find themselves in the sea. The fish live in the sea for three years. They swim far away from land. How do they find their way back? These fish have a wonderful sense of smell. They remember the scent of their journey easily because the river flowed to the sea and carried them there. After three years, most salmon swim toward the pools.

As soon as they reach a pool, the females lay their eggs. They lay their eggs near the edge of the water and cover them with sand. Soon the eggs hatch, and the pool is full of small fish, getting ready for the long journey out to the sea.

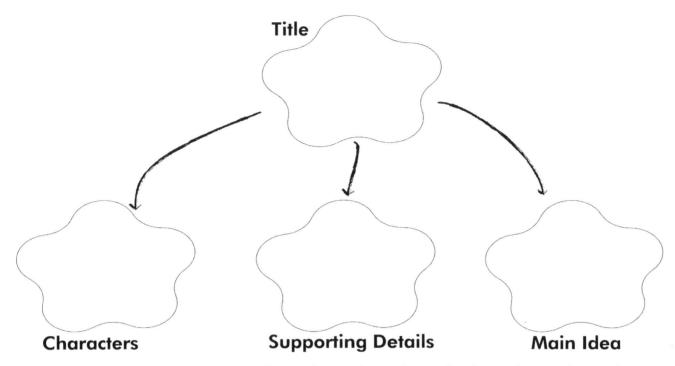

Characters   Supporting Details   Main Idea

6. Which detail in the paragraph tells us that salmon jump backward over the rocks?

   Ⓐ "When the baby fish are a few inches long, they begin to swim down the river."
   Ⓑ "Suddenly, they find themselves in the sea."
   Ⓒ "They swim far away from land."
   Ⓓ "As they grow bigger, they make their way towards the sea. They jump over rocks, often with their tails first."

7. According to the passage, how long do salmon live in the sea?

   Ⓐ six years
   Ⓑ three years
   Ⓒ one year
   Ⓓ five years

8. According to the text below, what is made out of orange flowers?

   Fruits begin to appear on the orange trees when they are three years old. Flowers and fruits may appear throughout the year. A very tasty and healthy kind of honey can be made from the orange flowers.

   Ⓐ A tasty but unhealthy kind of honey
   Ⓑ A tasty and healthy kind of honey
   Ⓒ A bad tasting, but healthy kind of honey
   Ⓓ Nothing is made out of the orange flowers.

Question 9 is based on the passage below

For a full, healthy, and useful life, sports are as important and necessary as work. They help us mentally, physically, and emotionally, and help us develop a healthy outlook towards life. Sports are very useful as a diversion of the mind. Most sports require skill and good judgment. Players not only develop their bodies but also their minds. Players must acquire the art of playing a game.

9. According to the passage, why are sports important?

   Ⓐ Sports help people mentally, physically, and emotionally.
   Ⓑ Sports do not require any special skills.
   Ⓒ Sports require players to develop their bodies only, not their minds.
   Ⓓ Sports are not useful.

10. What is the main idea of the below passage?

   Sports can develop character. The players must abide by the rules of the game. Any departure from following these rules means foul play. Every foul stroke in a game involves a penalty. Therefore, players play a fair game. Fair play is a noble and moral quality. Players become honest and punctual.

   Ⓐ Sports players are honest and punctual.
   Ⓑ Sports players must play a fair game.
   Ⓒ Sports players must abide by the rules.
   Ⓓ Sports can develop a strong character in players.

Question 11 is based on the passage below

There are three different kinds of oranges: the sweet or common orange, the mandarin orange, and the sour or bitter orange. One type of sweet orange is called the blood orange. It has a pulp with a deep red color. This type of orange is grown mostly in the Mediterranean region. Mandarin oranges are grown mostly in Florida. Sour oranges are grown almost everywhere, but Spain grows most of the sour oranges used for trade. These sour oranges are mainly used to make marmalade. But they can be put to many other interesting uses-from making medicine to creating perfumes. Oranges have many medicinal values. Oranges are the fruit with the greatest concentration of vitamin C. The thick, oily, and bitter skin does not allow any insects to get into an orange. Many kinds of useful oils can be extracted from this thick skin. Oranges are healthy and delicious.

11. Fill in the blank

   You will find that _____ are grown in Florida

Question 12 is based on the passage below

My cousin lives in California. Because that is such a long distance from Philadelphia, it takes a long time to drive there. This distance makes it so hard to visit her, and I miss her very much. Our parents think it is too hard to drive across the country to see each other, so I miss my cousin very much.

Because of this, I only see my cousin once a year. I want to see her more often so we can watch movies together, but our parents say no!

12. What is the main idea of the passage?

Ⓐ My cousin lives in California.
Ⓑ I want to see her more often, so we can see movies together; but, our parents say no!
Ⓒ I miss my cousin very much.
Ⓓ The distance makes it so hard to visit her, and I miss her very much.

Do NOT write your answers in this book. To open the answer sheet, scan the QR code or visit *lumoslearning.com/a/5e015*

Chapter 2 → Lesson 3: Text Relationships

Question 1 and 2 are based on the passage below

Once there was a severe drought. There was little water in Tony's well, and he didn't know what would happen to the fruit trees in his garden. Just then, he noticed three men looking intently at his house. He was certain that the three were planning to rob his house. He acted quickly. He shouted out to his son, "My son, due to the drought, money has become scarce. There are many thieves. Let us protect our valuables, and put all of our jewels in a box and throw them into the well. They will be safe there." He quickly told his son to put some large stones in a box and throw them into the well. The thieves heard the sound of the box falling into the well and were happy.

That night they came to the well. The box was heavy and had landed deep down in the well. To get it, they would have to take out some of the water. They started drawing water from the well and pouring it onto the ground. Tony had made arrangements to make sure that the water reached his fruit trees. He had channels leading from the well to each of the trees. By the time thieves found the box, they had drawn out enough water to water the trees. It was almost dawn. Tony sent for the soldiers, and just as the thieves were trying to open the box, they were caught red-handed.

1. What happens when the thieves started drawing water from the well and pouring it onto the ground?

    Ⓐ Tony started digging channels in the ground leading to his fruit trees.
    Ⓑ The thieves heard the sound of the box falling into the well.
    Ⓒ Tony's put all of the jewels into a box.
    Ⓓ Water reached the fruit trees through channels in the ground.

2. Why was there little water in the well at the beginning of the story?

    Ⓐ The thieves had drawn it all out and poured it onto the ground.
    Ⓑ There was a drought.
    Ⓒ Tony had used most of it to water his fruit trees.
    Ⓓ Tony's son drank nearly all of it.

> **Question 3 and 4 are based on the passage below**

The Glass Cupboard

There was a king who had a cupboard that was made entirely of glass. It was a special cupboard. It looked empty, but you could always take out anything you wanted. There was only one thing that had to be remembered. Whenever something was taken out of it, something else had to be put back in, although nobody knew why.

One day some thieves broke into the palace and stole the cupboard. "Now, we can have anything we want," they said. One of the thieves said, "I want a large bag of gold," and he opened the glass cupboard and got it. The other two did the same, and they, too, got exactly what they wanted. The thieves forgot one thing. Not one of them put anything back inside the cupboard.

This went on and on for weeks and months. At last, the leader of the thieves could bear it no longer. He took a hammer and smashed the glass cupboard into a million pieces, and then all three thieves fell down dead.

When the king returned home, he ordered his servants to search for the cupboard. When the servants found it and the dead thieves, they filled sixty great carts with the gold and took it back to the king. He said, "If those thieves had only put something back into the cupboard, they would be alive to this day."

He ordered his servants to collect all of the pieces of glass and melt into a globe of the world with all the countries on it; this was to remind himself and others, to give back something in return when someone shows an act of kindness or gives us something.

3. What happened when the king was away?

Ⓐ There was a storm, and it smashed the glass cupboard.
Ⓑ The palace servants accidentally broke the glass cupboard.
Ⓒ Some thieves broke into the palace and stole the glass cupboard.
Ⓓ None of the above

4. The reason that the king wanted a globe with all the countries of the world upon it was _____.

Ⓐ to sell it so he could afford to buy a new glass cupboard
Ⓑ to remind himself to give back something when someone gives him something
Ⓒ to remember the thieves that stole the glass cupboard
Ⓓ to prevent thieves from stealing from the palace

Question 5 and 6 are based on the story below

The Traveler

A weary traveler stopped at Sam's house and asked him for shelter for the night. Sam was a friendly soul. He not only agreed to let the traveler stay for the night; he decided to treat his guest to some curried chicken. So he bought a couple of chickens from the market and gave them to his wife to cook. Then he went off to buy some fruit.

Now Sam's wife could not resist food. She had a habit of eating as she cooked. So, as she cooked the meat, she smelled the rich steam and could not help tasting a piece. It was tender and delicious, and she decided to have another piece. Soon there was only a tiny bit left. Her little son, Kevin, ran into the kitchen. She gave him that little piece.

Kevin found it so tasty that he begged his mother for more. But there was no more chicken left. The traveler, who had gone to have a wash, returned. The woman heard him coming and had to think of a plan quickly. She began to scold her son loudly: "Your father has taught you a shameful and disgusting habit. Stop it, I tell you!" The traveler was curious. "What habit has his father taught the child?" he asked. "Oh," said the woman, "Whenever a guest arrives, my husband cuts off their ears and roasts them for my son to eat."

The traveler was shocked. He picked up his shoes and fled.

"Why has our guest left in such a hurry?" asked Sam when he came back.

"A fine guest indeed!" exclaimed his wife. "He snatched the chickens out of my pot and ran off with them!"

"The chickens!" exclaimed Sam. He ran after his guest, shouting. "Let me have one, at least; you may keep the other!" But his guest only ran faster!

5. Why did the traveler pick up his shoes and flee?

Ⓐ He disliked Sam's wife very much.
Ⓑ He thought Sam would be angry with him when he returned.
Ⓒ Sam's wife tricked him into thinking her husband would cut off his ears.
Ⓓ There were no chickens left to eat.

6. What happened as a result of Sam's wife's habit of eating as she cooked?

Ⓐ Travelers stopped by for dinner often.
Ⓑ Guests did not visit Sam and his wife's home.
Ⓒ Sam's wife put on weight.
Ⓓ There were no curried chickens left to eat.

> **Question 7 is based on the story below**

Do Your Best

Katie stood before the crowd, blushing and wringing her hands. She looked out and saw the room full of faces. Some she knew, and some she did not. But, they were all here to listen to her. Taking a deep breath, she opened her mouth, but no words came out. Tears formed in the corners of her eyes as she closed them.

With her eyes closed, she imagined her mother helping her get dressed and ready for tonight.

"Just do your best," is what her mother had told her.

She opened her eyes and found her mother's smiling face in the crowd. Relaxing, she took another deep breath and started singing. She did not stop until she finished, and the crowd was on their feet applauding.

After the show, she found her parents and her friends. They all had wonderful things to say about her song and how proud they were because she kept going even when it seemed like she might give up. She shrugged her shoulders and shared a smile with her mother.

"I just did my best," she answered.

7. Part A
What happened when Katie closed her eyes and remembered what her mother had told her?

Ⓐ She blushed and wringed her hands.
Ⓑ She started crying and ran off the stage.
Ⓒ She relaxed and started singing.
Ⓓ None of the above

Part B
What happened as a result of Katie's singing performance?

Ⓐ Katie gave up, because she couldn't keep going.
Ⓑ Her parents and friends told her they were proud of her.
Ⓒ Her mother helped her get dressed and ready.
Ⓓ None of the above

Question 8 is based on the story below

Late for School

Marrah heard the air in the bus brakes as she shoveled the rest of her breakfast into her mouth.

"You just missed the bus!" Marrah's mother yelled. "Why can't you ever be on time?"

"I'm sorry, Mom," Marrah sighed. She ran upstairs to her room so she could get her backpack, knowing she needed to hurry because her mother would have to take her to school.

"Let's go, Marrah!" Her mother called from downstairs. "You don't want to be late to school, too!"

Frantic now, Marrah lifted her sheets to look under them before dropping to her knees in front of her bed. She pushed mounds of clothes out of the way as she continued to search for her backpack.

"Marrah!" Her mother called again, and she could hear the impatience in her voice downstairs. She ran out of her room and leaned over the rail.

"I can't find my backpack!" she cried out.

"You mean this one?" Her mother pulled the bag from the floor beside her.

"Oh," she replied, her shoulders sagging as she walked down the stairs.

"Let's go to school, Marrah." Her mother said with a small smile on her face as they walked out the door.

8. Part A
The reason that Marrah missed the bus was that _____.

Ⓐ her mother didn't wake her up on time
Ⓑ she wasn't dressed yet
Ⓒ she couldn't find her backpack
Ⓓ she was still eating breakfast

Part B
Marrah looked under her sheets and pushed around mounds of clothes in her room, because _____.

Ⓐ she was looking for her backpack
Ⓑ she missed the bus
Ⓒ she couldn't decide what to wear to school
Ⓓ her mom told her to clean her room

Do NOT write your answers in this book. To open the answer sheet, scan the QR code or visit **lumoslearning.com/a/5e016**

Chapter 2 → Lesson 4: General Academic Vocabulary

1. **What is a reference source?**

   Ⓐ Sets of information that an author can base an article or story from such as almanacs, newspapers, and interviews
   Ⓑ The actual text that an author uses to write an article or story
   Ⓒ A set of information that is only valid in its primary form
   Ⓓ A set of information that is only valid in its secondary form

2. **What does a 'prompt' mean with respect to "language"?**

   Ⓐ A prompt details what the passage is about.
   Ⓑ A prompt is a basic idea of what to write about.
   Ⓒ A prompt forms the middle part of an essay.
   Ⓓ A prompt is the conclusion of the passage.

3. **What is personification?**

   Ⓐ A figure of speech where human characteristics are given to an animal or object
   Ⓑ A figure of speech where a word is used to describe a sound made by an object
   Ⓒ A figure of speech where a word or phrase means something different from what it says
   Ⓓ A figure of speech that draws a verbal picture by comparing two objects

4. **What is point of view?**

   Ⓐ The basis for which a story is formed
   Ⓑ The perspective from which the author tells the story
   Ⓒ The perspective from which the reader tells the story
   Ⓓ The sources where an author gains information to write a story

5. What is onomatopoeia?

Ⓐ A figure of speech where human characteristics are given to an animal or object
Ⓑ A figure of speech where a word is used to describe a sound made by an object
Ⓒ A figure of speech where a word or phrase means something different from what it says
Ⓓ A figure of speech that draws a verbal picture by comparing two objects

6. What is an idiom?

Ⓐ A figure of speech where human characteristics are given to an animal or object
Ⓑ A figure of speech where a word is used to describe a sound made by an object
Ⓒ A figure of speech where a word or phrase means something different from what it says
Ⓓ A figure of speech that draws a verbal picture by comparing two objects

7. What is the meaning of the underlined word?

Oranges have many medicinal values. Oranges are the fruit with the greatest concentration of vitamin C. The skin of the orange helps to keep the fruit inside from becoming damaged and to remain clean. The thick, oily, and bitter skin does not allow any insects to get into an orange. Many kinds of useful oils can be <u>extracted</u> from the thick skin. Oranges are healthy and delicious.

Ⓐ put in
Ⓑ concentrate
Ⓒ taken out
Ⓓ placed

Question 8 is based on the passage below

Salmon

A fish that is a great favorite with people is salmon. It begins its life in a small pool up a river. Far from the sea, the fish lays its eggs in a pool in the river. When the baby fish are a few inches long, they begin to swim down the river. As they grow bigger, they make their way towards the sea.

They jump over rocks, often with their tails first. Suddenly, they find themselves in the sea. The fish live in the sea for three years. They swim far away from land. How do they find their way back? These fish have a wonderful sense of smell. They remember the scent of their journey easily because the river flowed to the sea and carried them there. After three years, most salmon swim toward the pools.

As soon as they reach a pool, the females lay their eggs. They lay their eggs near the edge of the water and cover them with sand. Soon the eggs <u>hatch,</u> and the pool is full of small fish, getting ready for the long journey out to the sea.

8. What is the meaning of the underlined word?

   Ⓐ devise
   Ⓑ produce
   Ⓒ shade
   Ⓓ emerge

9. What is the meaning of the underlined word?

   We have been studying the <u>aftermath</u> of volcanos. Now I have to prepare an essay that includes this information.

   Ⓐ cause
   Ⓑ preparation
   Ⓒ consequences
   Ⓓ reason

10. What is the meaning of the underlined word?

    The American colonists have to formulate a plan to declare independence from Great Britain. Although the reasons vary, at the core, they want independence because they believe Great Britain takes away the rights of the colonists. But, without any real <u>specificity</u> of those reasons, other countries will have a difficult time supporting this new nation, and they must accumulate support if they are going to be able to break away.

    Ⓐ formulation
    Ⓑ creation
    Ⓒ definition
    Ⓓ reason

11. What is the meaning of the underlined word?

    The American colonists have to formulate a plan to declare independence from Great Britain. Although the reasons vary, at the core, they want independence because they believe Great Britain takes away the rights of the colonists. But, without any real specificity of those reasons, other countries will have a difficult time supporting this new nation, and they must <u>accumulate</u> support if they are going to be able to break away.

    Ⓐ gather
    Ⓑ create
    Ⓒ definition
    Ⓓ differ

Do NOT write your answers in this book. To open the answer sheet, scan the QR code or visit *lumoslearning.com/a/5e017*

Chapter 2 → Lesson 5: Text Structure

1. What is an index?

   Ⓐ It is a sequential arrangement of names, places, and topics along with the page numbers that they are discussed on.
   Ⓑ It is a list that helps in finding things pertaining to the topic faster.
   Ⓒ Both A and B
   Ⓓ None of the above

2. What is a glossary?

   Ⓐ A list of unusual words
   Ⓑ A list explaining or defining the difficult words and expressions used in the text
   Ⓒ A list of where a word can be found in the book
   Ⓓ Both B and C

Question 3 is based on the passage below

Salmon

A fish that is a great favorite with people is salmon. It begins its life in a small pool up a river. Far from the sea, the fish lays its eggs in a pool in the river. When the baby fish are a few inches long, they begin to swim down the river. As they grow bigger, they make their way towards the sea.

They jump over rocks, often with their tails first. Suddenly, they find themselves in the sea. The fish live in the sea for three years. They swim far away from land. How do they find their way back? These fish have a wonderful sense of smell. They remember the scent of their journey easily because the river flowed to the sea and carried them there. After three years, most salmon swim toward the pools.

As soon as they reach a pool, the females lay their eggs. They lay their eggs near the edge of the water and cover them with sand. Soon the eggs hatch, and the pool is full of small fish, getting ready for the long journey out to the sea.

3. What genre would the writing above be classified as?

   Ⓐ A nonfiction passage
   Ⓑ Informative writing
   Ⓒ Realistic fiction
   Ⓓ Both A and B

4. How is a Table of Contents helpful?

   Ⓐ It organizes the text into manageable passages.
   Ⓑ It lets the reader know where specific topics or chapters are and on what page number they begin.
   Ⓒ It lists and defines some of the most difficult words in the text.
   Ⓓ It is a list of unusual words.

5. Where is a Table of Contents located?

   Ⓐ It is located at the beginning of the text.
   Ⓑ It is located at the end of the text.
   Ⓒ It is located in the middle of the text.
   Ⓓ It is located at the beginning of each chapter of the text.

6. The heading of a letter usually includes which of the following?

   Ⓐ An address and date
   Ⓑ An introduction such as "Dear"
   Ⓒ A conclusion and signature
   Ⓓ None of the above

7. What is a comparison/contrast text structure?

   Ⓐ It is writing that looks at how two or more pieces of information are similar or different.
   Ⓑ It is writing that looks at how something occurs over a period of time.
   Ⓒ It is writing that looks at why something happened and what else occurred as a result.
   Ⓓ It is writing that looks at answers to different dilemmas.

8. What is a problem/solution text structure?

   Ⓐ It is writing that looks at how two or more pieces of information are similar or different.
   Ⓑ It is writing that looks at how something occurs over a period of time.
   Ⓒ It is writing that looks at why something happened and what else occurred as a result.
   Ⓓ It is writing that looks at answers to different dilemmas.

9. What type of text structure would best address this information?

I have been studying the water shortage crisis in several states. My report will include the facts I have found as well as various prevention techniques for future droughts.

Ⓐ cause and effect
Ⓑ problem and solution
Ⓒ chronological order
Ⓓ compare and contrast

10. What type of text structure would best address this information?

We have been studying the aftermath of volcanoes. Now I have to prepare an essay that includes this information.

Ⓐ cause and effect
Ⓑ problem and solution
Ⓒ chronological order
Ⓓ compare and contrast

11. What type of text structure would best address this information?

I want to study the order of events leading up to the American Revolution. I think I should start my research in the school library.

Ⓐ cause and effect
Ⓑ problem and solution
Ⓒ chronological order
Ⓓ compare and contrast

Do NOT write your answers in this book. To open the answer sheet, scan the QR code or visit **lumoslearning.com/a/5e018**

Chapter 2 → Lesson 6: Point of View

1. Identify the point of view used in the paragraph below.

Mary sat in front of Peter in the classroom. She had two long blonde braids in the back of her hair. Peter reached out and tugged on her braids. Mary turned around and swatted Peter with her notebook.

Ⓐ first person
Ⓑ third person
Ⓒ none of the above

2. Identify the point of view used in the paragraph below.

It was a cool, crisp morning. Lucy threw her backpack over her shoulders, jumped on her bicycle, and pedaled down Pine Street. Her tires made soft crunching noises as she drove through piles of brown, yellow, and orange leaves.

Ⓐ first person
Ⓑ second person
Ⓒ third person
Ⓓ none of the above

3. Identify the point of view used in the paragraph below.

Mrs. Davis lived in a great big apartment on the top floor of her building. As I walked into her spacious, clean apartment, I noticed fine, leather furniture, and expensive works of art. Mrs. Davis sat up in her large, king-size bed wearing a beautiful, silk robe and smiled at me. She looked like she felt better than she had the last time I visited.

Ⓐ first person
Ⓑ second person
Ⓒ third person
Ⓓ none of the above

4. Identify the point of view of the paragraph below.

At the bakery, Vince, the baker, was getting the muffins ready for baking. He mixed up flour, sugar, milk, and blueberries. He poured the mixture into a muffin pan and placed it into the oven. Then, he heard one of his employees call him from the front of the store. "A lady wants six blueberry muffins!" "Ok," Vince called back, "I'll have them ready in ten minutes!"

Ⓐ first person
Ⓑ second person
Ⓒ third person
Ⓓ none of the above

5. Identify the point of view in the sentences below.

I took one look at the hideous creature and ran away as fast as I could. I had never been so scared in my whole life!

Ⓐ first person
Ⓑ second person
Ⓒ third person
Ⓓ none of the above

6. Identify the point of view in the paragraph below.

Kara's mother wakes up at 5:30 A.M. every morning so that she'll have time to study for her college classes. This is the only time that she has to study before she has to go to work. She takes college classes two nights a week. Every weekend, she volunteers at the local homeless shelter. She has been helping out there for the past three years.

Ⓐ first person
Ⓑ second person
Ⓒ third person
Ⓓ none of the above

7. Identify the point of view in the paragraph below.

Victor took off his reading glasses and rubbed his eyes. He picked up his walking cane. Then he slowly used the cane to help himself up from the bench. Every day, it takes him a little bit longer to stand up. Every day, it becomes more difficult for him to walk.

Ⓐ first person
Ⓑ second person
Ⓒ third person
Ⓓ none of the above

8. Identify the point of view in the paragraph below.

Before each practice starts, make sure that everyone on your team is wearing the proper equipment. Be sure that everyone is wearing athletic shoes and a helmet. It's also important to remind your teammates to remove any jewelry, because it could injure another player. You should also have a first-aid kit on hand.

Ⓐ first person
Ⓑ second person
Ⓒ third person
Ⓓ none of the above

9. Identify the point of view in the sentences below.

Corky waddled toward the lake. When he reached the water, he flapped his wings, quacked, and jumped in.

Ⓐ first person
Ⓑ second person
Ⓒ third person
Ⓓ none of the above

10. Identify the point of view in the paragraph below.

Once you have your computer desk assembled, the next thing to decide is where to put it. A desktop computer requires electricity, so you will need to make sure you choose a spot where there's an electrical outlet available.

Ⓐ first person
Ⓑ second person
Ⓒ third person
Ⓓ none of the above

Do NOT write your answers in this book. To open the answer sheet, scan the QR code or visit **lumoslearning.com/a/5e019**

Chapter 2 → Lesson 7: Locating Answers

Question 1 is based on the poem below

What is this life if, full of care,
We have no time to stand and stare?

No time to stand beneath the boughs
And stare as long as sheep or cows.

No time to see, when woods we pass,
Where squirrels hide their nuts in grass

No time to see, in broad daylight,
Streams full of stars, like skies at night.

No time to turn at Beauty's glance,
And watch her feet, how they can dance.

No time to wait till her mouth can
Enrich that smile her eyes began.

A poor life if, full of care,
We have no time to stand and stare.
- W. H. Davies

1. If you had to research the poet above, where would you look for information?

Ⓐ in the library
Ⓑ on the Internet
Ⓒ in a book about different poets
Ⓓ all of the above

2. Where might you find the passage below?

   I went for a run this morning. Although I usually run in the evening, I decided to go in the morning because of the weather. It has been so hot this summer, so hot in fact, that I cannot run in the evening. Therefore, until we have cooler weather, I will continue to enjoy a morning run.

   Ⓐ You might find it in a newspaper.
   Ⓑ You might find it on the Internet.
   Ⓒ You might find it in a journal or diary.
   Ⓓ You might find it in a book report.

3. If you wanted to write a report about a famous author, where would be the best place to look for information?

   Ⓐ a biography or autobiography of the author
   Ⓑ the newspaper
   Ⓒ the Internet
   Ⓓ both A & C

4. Where would you find the meaning of the word 'thespian'?

   Ⓐ in an encyclopedia
   Ⓑ in a dictionary
   Ⓒ in a journal
   Ⓓ in an almanac

5. Where could you read the weather forecast for tomorrow?

   Ⓐ dictionary
   Ⓑ almanac
   Ⓒ newspaper
   Ⓓ encyclopedia

6. Where would you best look for a synonym for the word procrastinate?

   Ⓐ thesaurus
   Ⓑ atlas
   Ⓒ almanac
   Ⓓ dictionary

7. You want to find out the neighboring countries of France. What reference material should you use?

    Ⓐ an almanac
    Ⓑ an atlas
    Ⓒ a newspaper
    Ⓓ a dictionary

8. Read each of the statement and match it with the place in which you can locate it in a text book

	Table of Contents	Glossary	Index	Copyright page
Where would you look to locate a chapter on the Civil War?	○	○	○	○
Where would you look to locate the definition of a key word?	○	○	○	○
Where would you look to locate the alphabetical list of important topics?	○	○	○	○
Where would you look to locate when the book was published?	○	○	○	○

9. In a textbook, where can additional information such as additional charts and graphs be found?

    Ⓐ Appendix
    Ⓑ Index
    Ⓒ Table of Contents
    Ⓓ Glossary

Chapter 2 → Lesson 8: Using Evidence to Support Claims

Question 1 and 2 are based on the story below

The Orange

1. Even though no one knows exactly where oranges come from, Southeast Asia is believed to be their first home. They are grown today in most of the warmer parts of the world. The ancient Greeks and Romans knew about oranges. It is possible that oranges were carried from India to Western Asia and then to Europe.

2. The Spaniards took the sour oranges to the West Indies and from there to Florida, in America. Today, oranges are the most important fresh fruit in international trade. There are three different kinds of oranges: the sweet or common orange, the mandarin orange, and the sour or bitter orange.

3. One type of sweet orange is called the blood orange. It has a pulp with a deep red color. This type of orange is grown mostly in the Mediterranean region. Mandarin oranges are mainly found in Florida. Sour oranges are grown almost everywhere, with Spain having the greatest number used for trade. These sour oranges are generally used to make marmalade.

4. However, they can be put to many other interesting uses, from making medicine to creating perfumes. Oranges have many medicinal values. Oranges are the fruit with the greatest concentration of vitamin C. The skin of the orange helps to keep the fruit inside from becoming damaged and to remain clean. The thick, oily, and bitter skin does not allow any insects to get into an orange. Many kinds of useful oils can be extracted from the thick skin. Oranges are healthy and delicious.

1. Which paragraph discusses the types of oranges?

   Ⓐ paragraph one
   Ⓑ paragraph two
   Ⓒ paragraph three
   Ⓓ both B and C

2. Which paragraph discusses the health value of oranges?

Ⓐ paragraph one
Ⓑ paragraph two
Ⓒ paragraph three
Ⓓ paragraph four

Question 3 is based on the passage below.

Salmon

A fish that is a great favorite with people is salmon. It begins its life in a small pool up a river. Far from the sea, the fish lays its eggs in a pool in the river. When the baby fish are a few inches long, they begin to swim down the river. As they grow bigger, they make their way towards the sea.

They jump over rocks, often with their tails first. Suddenly, they find themselves in the sea. The fish live in the sea for three years. They swim far away from land. How do they find their way back? These fish have a wonderful sense of smell. They remember the scent of their journey easily because the river flowed to the sea and carried them there. After three years, most salmon swim toward the pools.

As soon as they reach a pool, the females lay their eggs. They lay their eggs near the edge of the water and cover them with sand. Soon the eggs hatch, and the pool is full of small fish, getting ready for the long journey out to the sea.

3. Which sentence in the first paragraph discusses where salmon begin their lives?

Ⓐ sentence one
Ⓑ sentence two
Ⓒ sentence three
Ⓓ sentence four

4. Which sentence indicates how long the author will continue to run in the morning time?

I went for a run this morning. Although I usually run in the evening, I decided to go in the morning because of the weather. It has been so hot this summer, so hot in fact, that I cannot run in the evening. Therefore, until we have cooler weather, I will continue to enjoy a morning run.

Ⓐ one
Ⓑ two
Ⓒ three
Ⓓ four

Question 5 is based on the passage below

Sports can develop character. The players must abide by the rules of the game. Any departure from following these rules means foul play. Every foul stroke in a game involves a penalty. Therefore, players play a fair game. Fair play is a noble and moral quality.

Players become honest and punctual. The player develops the sportsman's spirit. Defeat does not dishearten a true sportsman. He does not feel over-excited if he wins a match. He learns to take both victory and defeat in stride. He never strikes an adversary.

5. Read the above paragraphs and identify the main idea.

Ⓐ Every foul stroke in a game involves a penalty.
Ⓑ Sports develop a player's character.
Ⓒ The players have to abide by the rules of the game.
Ⓓ Any departure from these rules means foul play.

Question 6-8 are based on the passage below

My mother works extremely hard as a nurse. Each day she gives her all, and when she comes home, she is dog tired. I like to help her take a load off, so I try and make dinner for her. I also clean the house and mow the yard outside. Today was even more difficult, though. It rained like cats and dogs all afternoon, so I couldn't take care of the yard. Then, when I came inside to clean, I realized the kitchen sink was clogged, and the washing machine seemed broken. I couldn't catch a break! By the time Mom came home, I had given up, called a plumber, and ordered a pizza. It's a good thing my mom always taught me that where there is a will, there is a way!

6. Which sentence explains why today was difficult?

Ⓐ two
Ⓑ four
Ⓒ six
Ⓓ eight

7. Which sentence explains what happened when the author tried to clean?

Ⓐ one
Ⓑ three
Ⓒ five
Ⓓ seven

8. Which detail explains why the mother is so tired?

   Ⓐ She works hard as a nurse.
   Ⓑ She has to clean the house.
   Ⓒ She has to do the laundry.
   Ⓓ She has to mow the lawn.

9. According the graph, which type of orange is the most popular?

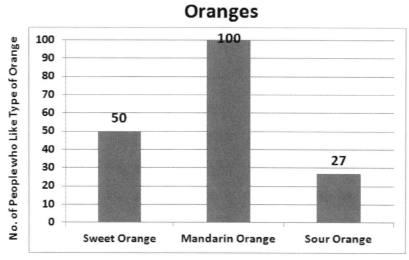

   Ⓐ Sweet Orange
   Ⓑ Mandarin Orange
   Ⓒ Sour Orange

10. Select the phrase that best completes the sentence.

    Evidence to support details can be found _____.

    Ⓐ in the text and title only
    Ⓑ in the text only
    Ⓒ in the text, illustrations, graphs, and headings
    Ⓓ in the conclusion

11. **Select the phrase that best completes the sentence.**

    Informational text is richer and more powerful when _____.

    Ⓐ it is filled with vivid language
    Ⓑ it uses action verbs
    Ⓒ it is filled with details
    Ⓓ it is filled with evidence to support claims

Do NOT write your answers in this book. To open the answer sheet, scan the QR code or visit *lumoslearning.com/a/5e021*

Chapter 2 → Lesson 9: Integrating Information

1. **In which situation would you possibly need to read multiple texts?**

   Ⓐ to locate an answer to a question
   Ⓑ to write or speak about a topic knowledgeably
   Ⓒ to fully understand a historical or scientific concept
   Ⓓ all of the above

2. **Fill in the blank after choosing the correct option from among the 4 options given below**
   If you are studying World War II, you might _____.

   Ⓐ read a chapter from your social studies textbook about World War II
   Ⓑ look at a book of photographs from the war
   Ⓒ read a magazine article written by someone who fought in the war
   Ⓓ all of the above

3. **If you wanted to start a recycling club at your school, where could you learn more information?**

   Ⓐ Go to the library and read books about recycling.
   Ⓑ Search the Internet to find websites about recycling.
   Ⓒ Both A and B
   Ⓓ None of the above

4. **In which of the following texts would an author most likely use a "subjective" point of view?**

   Ⓐ a chapter in a history textbook
   Ⓑ a letter which was written by a soldier to his father found in the war
   Ⓒ a memoir written years after the war by a woman whose son died in the war
   Ⓓ both b and c

5. In which of the following texts would an author most likely use an "objective" point of view?

   Ⓐ a newspaper article about how the American Red Cross helps during natural disaster
   Ⓑ a book of photographs of natural disasters
   Ⓒ Both A and B
   Ⓓ None of the above

6. Choose the sentence below that is written in a subjective point of view.

   Suppose your parents asked you to attend your little sister's softball game.

   Ⓐ The final score was 12 to 11.
   Ⓑ The game was really boring.
   Ⓒ My sister's team won the game.
   Ⓓ None of the above

Question 7-9 are based on the passage below

Lost in the Woods

One day, a little girl named Tessa asked her mom if she could invite her friend Katelyn over for a sleepover. Her mom agreed. When Katelyn arrived at Tessa's house the next afternoon, the girls decided to go exploring in the woods close to Tessa's house. When the girls did not come back inside the house after a while, Tessa's mom decided to go looking for them. She walked to the edge of the woods and called out to them, but she heard no reply. After looking for them for about an hour, she decided to call 911.

Within hours, nearly 100 police officers and volunteers were searching for them in the woods. One of the officers brought Nickel, a search-and-rescue dog. Tessa's mom let the dog sniff one of Tessa's shirts so the dog could track the girl's scent. Nickel and her handler set off to look for the girls.

As they were walking down a trail, Nickel suddenly veered off the trail and headed downhill. Nickel led the volunteers down an embankment, and under a tree, they found the two girls scared but unhurt. In less than an hour, Tessa and Katelyn were back with their relieved families. The girls were thankful Nickel had found them. Nickel went home to wait for his next mission.

SAR Dogs

Search-and-rescue (SAR) dogs are special dogs with an acute sense of smell that are called in when a person is lost or trapped. SAR dogs search in remote areas and in places struck by natural disasters such as earthquakes, tornadoes, and hurricanes. SAR dogs are very effective and can often locate people when many volunteers can't.

LumosLearning.com

Dogs make great searchers because of their powerful sense of smell. SAR dogs are trained to use their incredible sense of smell to search for people.

In 2010, SAR dogs from the United States found people trapped in the rubble after a devastating earthquake in Haiti. In 2012, SAR dogs helped locate people who were trapped in their homes after Hurricane Sandy hit the East Coast. These are only a few instances when SAR dogs have helped people.

7. What is the purpose of the second passage "SAR Dogs?"

Ⓐ To teach readers about earthquakes
Ⓑ To provide readers with information about search-and-rescue dogs
Ⓒ To give examples of types of search-and-rescue dogs
Ⓓ To tell a story about a rescue effort

8. Part A
What is the girls' attitude toward SAR dogs?

Ⓐ They are scared of them.
Ⓑ They are angry at them.
Ⓒ They are thankful for them.
Ⓓ They make them sad.

Part B
How does information from "SAR Dogs" add to your understanding of the story "Lost in the Woods?"

Ⓐ It explains that the dogs' sense of smell helps them find people.
Ⓑ It helps the reader to understand the setting of the story.
Ⓒ It helps the reader to get to know the characters better.
Ⓓ It informs the reader about natural disasters of the past.

9. From which point of view is SAR Dogs told?

Ⓐ first person
Ⓑ objective
Ⓒ subjective
Ⓓ none of the above

End of Reading Informational Text

Chapter 3
Language

Do NOT write your answers in this book. To open the answer sheet, scan the QR code or visit *lumoslearning.com/a/5e022*

Lesson 1: Pronoun-Antecedent Agreement

1. Select the correct antecedent to complete the sentence.

   Someone has dropped _____ wallet.

   Ⓐ his
   Ⓑ her
   Ⓒ their
   Ⓓ his or her

2. Select the word that best completes the sentence.

   If a singular pronoun is used, a _____ antecedent must be used.

   Ⓐ singular
   Ⓑ plural
   Ⓒ advanced
   Ⓓ regular

3. Which sentence has the correct pronoun and antecedent usage?

   Ⓐ Margaret called their mother to come to the mall.
   Ⓑ Bill picked up a new tool for his garage today.
   Ⓒ This is Kelsey's house.
   Ⓓ Jose and his friends brought his phones with them.

4. Select the correct antecedent to complete the sentence.

   Fruits begin to appear on the orange trees when they are three years old. Flowers and fruits may appear throughout the year. A very tasty and healthy kind of honey can be made from _____.

   Ⓐ it
   Ⓑ her
   Ⓒ they
   Ⓓ them

5. Which sentence has a correct pronoun and antecedent usage?

   Ⓐ My grandmother came to visit me and my sister to the mall, and she took us to the mall.
   Ⓑ My grandmother came to visit my sister and I to the mall, and she took us to the mall.
   Ⓒ My grandmother came to visit my sister and me, and she took us to the mall.
   Ⓓ None of these sentences are correct.

6. Select the word that correctly completes the sentence.

   In order to finish the Halloween costume, Alyssa and _____ went to the mall.

   Ⓐ me
   Ⓑ her
   Ⓒ I
   Ⓓ them

7. According to pronoun rules, when do you use the subject pronoun 'I' in a compound sentence?

   Ⓐ You use it before the other pronoun or noun.
   Ⓑ You use it after the other pronoun or noun.
   Ⓒ You use it after the adjective.
   Ⓓ You use it after the verb.

8. Select the correct antecedent to complete the sentence.

   My brother and I went to the movies, and we enjoyed____.

   Ⓐ it
   Ⓑ they
   Ⓒ those
   Ⓓ them

9. Select the correct antecedent to complete the sentence.

   Billy and I play together every day. Yesterday, his mother came over and asked _____ if we wanted to eat dinner together. We said yes.

   Ⓐ he and I
   Ⓑ him and me
   Ⓒ he and me
   Ⓓ him and I

10. Which sentence has the correct pronoun and antecedent usage?

Ⓐ My brother and I are going to rebuild our engine.
Ⓑ My brother and I are going to rebuild our engine.
Ⓒ Me and my brother are going to rebuild our engine.
Ⓓ Myself and my brother are going to rebuild our engine.

11. Fill in the blank with the correct antecedent to complete the sentence.

My big brother just got ___ first car, so perhaps he and I can finally spend some time together!

12. Which sentence has the correct pronoun and antecedent usage?

Ⓐ A fish that is a great favorite with people is salmon. They begins its life in a small pool up a river.
Ⓑ A fish that is a great favorite with people is salmon. Them begins its life in a small pool up a river.
Ⓒ A fish that is a great favorite with people is salmon. It begins its life in a small pool up a river.
Ⓓ A fish that is a great favorite with people is salmon. He begins its life in a small pool up a river.

13. Which sentence has the correct pronoun and antecedent usage?

Ⓐ So as Sally cooked the meat, either smelled the rich steam and could not help tasting a piece.
Ⓑ So as Sally cooked the meat, them smelled the rich steam and could not help tasting a piece.
Ⓒ So as Sally cooked the meat, her smelled the rich steam and could not help tasting a piece.
Ⓓ So as Sally cooked the meat, she smelled the rich steam and could not help tasting a piece.

Do NOT write your answers in this book. To open the answer sheet, scan the QR code or visit *lumoslearning.com/a/5e023*

Chapter 3 → Lesson 2: Prepositional Phrases

1. **Select the phrase that best completes the sentence.**

   Prepositions are _____.

   Ⓐ words that introduce or connect
   Ⓑ words that confuse
   Ⓒ words that show action
   Ⓓ words that end a sentence

2. **Identify the preposition in the below sentence.**

   We met at the loud concert.

   Ⓐ we
   Ⓑ met
   Ⓒ at
   Ⓓ concert

3. **Identify the object of the preposition in the below sentence.**

   We met at the loud concert.

   Ⓐ we
   Ⓑ met
   Ⓒ at
   Ⓓ concert

4. Select the phrase that best completes the below sentence.

The object of a preposition is _____.

- Ⓐ the actual preposition
- Ⓑ the noun or pronoun that follows the preposition
- Ⓒ a word that identifies
- Ⓓ a word that shows direction

5. Select the phrase that best completes the below sentence.

A prepositional phrase always _____.

- Ⓐ begins with a preposition
- Ⓑ ends with a preposition
- Ⓒ has a preposition in the middle
- Ⓓ none of the above

6. Identify the preposition in the below sentence.

My mother plants orange trees in the backyard that give us wonderful fruit.

- Ⓐ plants
- Ⓑ in
- Ⓒ backyard
- Ⓓ wonderful

7. Identify the object of the preposition in the below sentence.

My mother plants orange trees in the backyard that give us wonderful fruit.

- Ⓐ plants
- Ⓑ in
- Ⓒ backyard
- Ⓓ wonderful

8. Identify the preposition in the below sentence.

Grandpa drives a yellow school bus each morning to the school.

- Ⓐ drives
- Ⓑ bus
- Ⓒ to
- Ⓓ school

9. Identify the prepositional phrase in the below sentence.

Grandpa drives a yellow school bus each morning to the school.

Ⓐ drives a
Ⓑ yellow school bus
Ⓒ to the school
Ⓓ to school

10. Identify the preposition in the below sentence.

The pen is behind the chair.

Ⓐ pen
Ⓑ behind
Ⓒ chair
Ⓓ is

11. Fill in the blank with the preposition that best completes the sentence.

I am dealing with someone who keeps stealing my lunch money _____ school.

12. Select the preposition that best completes the sentence by circling it.

Tomorrow will be the third day we have lived ____ the new house.

Ⓐ in
Ⓑ on
Ⓒ at
Ⓓ with

> Do NOT write your answers in this book. To open the answer sheet, scan the QR code or visit **lumoslearning.com/a/5e024**

Chapter 3 → Lesson 3: Verbs

1. **What is the correct way to write the underlined verb?**

   Mrs. Smith <u>teach</u> us math this year.

   Ⓐ teaches
   Ⓑ taught
   Ⓒ teaching
   Ⓓ teached

2. **In which sentence is the verb *have* used correctly?**

   Ⓐ Emily have a wonderful dinner last night.
   Ⓑ I have lemon cake for dessert tomorrow.
   Ⓒ She have chocolate chip cookies today.
   Ⓓ I have a brownie for a snack.

3. **What is the correct way to write the underlined verb?**

   My uncle <u>have</u> the greatest music collection, and I cannot wait to borrow some of his songs!

   Ⓐ had
   Ⓑ has
   Ⓒ have
   Ⓓ having

4. **In which sentence is the verb *sing* used correctly?**

   Ⓐ Jose wants to sing at the end of the year talent show.
   Ⓑ Bill sing every Friday night.
   Ⓒ Last week, Jimmy sing at Sue's party.
   Ⓓ My favorite part of the night was sing with everyone on the hayride.

5. In which of the following sentences can the verb *climbing* be used correctly?

Ⓐ I _____ the mountain last year.
Ⓑ My mother and I _____ three flights of stairs.
Ⓒ Maggie went rock _____ at the gym yesterday.
Ⓓ Yesterday, my sister said I could _____ to the top of the highest hill.

6. What is the correct way to write the underlined verb?

Gerry and I <u>be</u> going fishing tomorrow to catch dinner for our family.

Ⓐ been
Ⓑ are
Ⓒ am
Ⓓ is

7. What is the correct way to write the underlined verb?

Last year, I <u>dance</u> a solo at my end of the year recital.

Ⓐ dancing
Ⓑ dances
Ⓒ dance
Ⓓ danced

8. In which sentence is the verb *make* used correctly?

Ⓐ I make cupcakes right now.
Ⓑ I usually make dinner for my family.
Ⓒ My mother make homemade ice cream tonight.
Ⓓ Billy make dinner for his family tonight.

9. What is the correct way to write the underlined verb?

A weary traveler <u>visit</u> my farm yesterday.

Ⓐ visiting
Ⓑ visited
Ⓒ visits
Ⓓ visit

10. What is the correct way to write the underlined verb in the sentence?

The two brothers <u>fight</u> yesterday, but today they both apologized.

- Ⓐ fighting
- Ⓑ fights
- Ⓒ fought
- Ⓓ fighted

11. What is the correct way to write the underlined verb? Enter your answer in the box given below.

Fruits <u>beginning</u> to appear on the orange trees when they are three years old.

12. What is the correct way to write the underlined verb? Enter your answer in the box given below.

Each day she <u>giving</u> her all, and when she comes home she is dog tired.

Do NOT write your answers in this book. To open the answer sheet, scan the QR code or visit *lumoslearning.com/a/5e025*

Chapter 3 → Lesson 4: Subject-Verb Agreement

1. Select the correct form of the verb to complete the below sentence.

   The video game my sister _____ _____ broke, and it is all her fault.

   Ⓐ are playing
   Ⓑ were playing
   Ⓒ was playing
   Ⓓ will play

2. Select the correct subject to complete the below sentence.

   _____ are the reason we are late today.

   Ⓐ She
   Ⓑ They
   Ⓒ He
   Ⓓ Her

3. Select the correct subject to complete the below sentence.

   Her father is cooking breakfast before school tomorrow morning. The menu will include eggs, bacon, and biscuits. My sister and _____ cannot wait to wake up and eat!

   Ⓐ I
   Ⓑ we
   Ⓒ me
   Ⓓ None of the above

LumosLearning.com

4. Select the correct verb to complete the below sentence.

He _____ the chickens out of the yard and ran off with them!

Ⓐ snatch
Ⓑ snatched
Ⓒ snatching
Ⓓ snatcher

5. Select the correct tense of the verb to complete the below sentence.

The traveler, who had gone to have a wash, _____.

Ⓐ returned
Ⓑ has returns
Ⓒ returning
Ⓓ return

6. Identify the correct verb phrase from the below sentence.

The skateboarding show really _____ soon.

Ⓐ be starting
Ⓑ started
Ⓒ should be starting
Ⓓ start

7. Select the correct subject to complete the below sentence.

_____ performed beautifully yesterday, and I'm sure they will again today.

Ⓐ Them choir
Ⓑ They choir
Ⓒ The choir
Ⓓ There choir

8. Select the correct subject to complete the below sentence.

My mother and I were racing against each other in the video game, and she kept winning. Now, _____ and my brother are going to compete!

Ⓐ I
Ⓑ she
Ⓒ her
Ⓓ None of the above

9. Select the correct verb to complete the below sentence.

   One type of sweet orange _____ the blood orange.

   Ⓐ called
   Ⓑ call
   Ⓒ is called
   Ⓓ is call

10. Which two verb tenses, in the given order, are used in the below sentences?

    She danced so beautifully. She dances so beautifully.

    Ⓐ present, past
    Ⓑ past, present
    Ⓒ present, future
    Ⓓ future, perfect

11. Identify the verb phrase in the below sentence.

    Although she has been able to practice, she can never perfect the backflip.

    Enter your answer in the box given below.

12. What tense are the verbs in this below lines?

    As salmon grow bigger, they make their way towards the sea. They jump over rocks, often with their tails first. Suddenly, they find themselves in the sea.

    Enter your answer in the box given below.

Do NOT write your answers in this book. To open the answer sheet, scan the QR code or visit *lumoslearning.com/a/5e026*

Chapter 3 → Lesson 5: Adjectives and Adverbs

1. **These words are used to modify and describe nouns and pronouns.**

   Ⓐ Adjectives
   Ⓑ Adverbs
   Ⓒ Nouns
   Ⓓ Verbs

2. **These words are used to modify or describe verbs or adverbs.**

   Ⓐ Adjectives
   Ⓑ Adverbs
   Ⓒ Nouns
   Ⓓ Verbs

3. **What part of speech is the underlined word in the below sentence?**

   She teaches her class <u>patiently</u>.

   Ⓐ Noun
   Ⓑ Verb
   Ⓒ Adjective
   Ⓓ Adverb

4. **What part of speech is the underlined word in the sentence below?**

   She is a <u>patient</u> teacher.

   Ⓐ Noun
   Ⓑ Verb
   Ⓒ Adjective
   Ⓓ Adverb

5. **Which underlined word is not an adjective?**

   This exciting movie is wonderful. The plot is quite suspenseful. Several parts are also very funny, and the humor adds much to the movie.

   Ⓐ exciting
   Ⓑ suspenseful
   Ⓒ several
   Ⓓ humor

6. **Select the answer that has the correct adjectives in the correct order to complete the sentence.**

   My cousin used to be one of the _____ basketball players in the world. Now, there are only two players that are _____ than him.

   Ⓐ taller, tallest
   Ⓑ tallest, taller
   Ⓒ most tall, more tall
   Ⓓ tallest, more tall

7. **What part of speech is the underlined word in the sentence?**

   My brother is a good driver. He drives very well.

   Ⓐ adjective
   Ⓑ noun
   Ⓒ adverb
   Ⓓ verb

8. **What is the underlined word in the sentence?**

   Orange trees produce wonderful fruit and flowers all year long.

   Ⓐ adjective
   Ⓑ noun
   Ⓒ adverb
   Ⓓ verb

9. Select the answer that has the correct adjectives in the correct order to complete the sentence.

She makes the most _____ chocolate chip cookies. They are so good that the most _____ bakery in the nation wants her recipe.

Ⓐ delicious, famous
Ⓑ famous, delicious
Ⓒ deliciouser, famouser
Ⓓ delicious, all famous

10. Which underlined word is NOT an adjective?

This is the craziest movie I have seen in a long time. So far it has had the ugliest monsters, the scariest vampires, and the strangest werewolves.

Ⓐ craziest
Ⓑ ugliest
Ⓒ scariest
Ⓓ werewolves

11. What part of speech is the underlined word in the above sentence? Enter your answer in the box given below.

Robin works here.

12. Select the word that best completes the sentence.

When you want to describe how you feel, you should use an _____.

Ⓐ adjective
Ⓑ adverb
Ⓒ noun
Ⓓ verb

Chapter 3 → Lesson 6: Correlative Conjunctions

1. Which set of conjunctions correctly completes the sentence?

   Danielle wants _____ pizza _____ pasta for lunch, because she doesn't like Italian food.

   Ⓐ either, or
   Ⓑ neither, and
   Ⓒ neither, nor
   Ⓓ either, and

2. Which set of conjunctions correctly completes the sentence?

   I can't decide _____ I should take Spanish class next year _____ German class.

   Ⓐ either, or
   Ⓑ whether, or
   Ⓒ neither, nor
   Ⓓ whether, nor

3. Which set of conjunctions correctly completes the sentence?

   _____ my mom _____ my dad can take me to the library.

   Ⓐ Whether, or
   Ⓑ Neither, nor
   Ⓒ Either, nor
   Ⓓ Whether, nor

4. Which set of conjunctions correctly completes the sentence?

_____ you give back my sweater you borrowed last week, _____ I won't loan you my new dress.

Ⓐ Either, or
Ⓑ Neither, nor
Ⓒ Whether, or
Ⓓ Either, nor

5. Which set of conjunctions correctly completes the sentence?

_____ we go to the mountains for vacation _____ to the beach, I'll be happy.

Ⓐ Either, nor
Ⓑ Either, or
Ⓒ Neither, nor
Ⓓ Whether, or

6. Which set of conjunctions correctly completes the sentence?

_____ we can go for a walk in the park tomorrow afternoon, _____ we can go watch a ballgame instead.

Ⓐ Either, or
Ⓑ Either, nor
Ⓒ Neither, nor
Ⓓ Whether, or

7. Which set of conjunctions correctly completes the sentence?

I'm sorry, but I have _____ the money _____ the time to shop for new clothes right now.

Ⓐ either, or
Ⓑ either, whether
Ⓒ neither, nor
Ⓓ whether, or

8. Which set of conjunctions correctly completes the sentence?

I can't decide _____ to join the marching band next year _____ try out for the football team.

Ⓐ whether, nor
Ⓑ neither, or
Ⓒ neither, nor
Ⓓ whether, or

9. Which set of conjunctions correctly completes the sentence?

_____ Donna _____ Natalie won the art contest, even though they are both very talented.

Ⓐ Either, or
Ⓑ Neither, or
Ⓒ Neither, nor
Ⓓ Whether, or

10. Which of the following are pairs of correlative conjunctions?

Ⓐ either, or
Ⓑ neither, nor
Ⓒ whether, or
Ⓓ all of the above

Do NOT write your answers in this book. To open the answer sheet, scan the QR code or visit *lumoslearning.com/a/5e028*

Chapter 3 → Lesson 7: Capitalization

1. Select the sentence that uses capital letters correctly.

   Ⓐ My Cat, Katie, is black and white.
   Ⓑ My cat, Katie, is black and white.
   Ⓒ my Cat, Katie, is black and white.
   Ⓓ My cat, katie, is black and white.

2. Select the sentence that uses capital letters correctly.

   Ⓐ Nana has two Dogs, named Hank and Sugar, who love the Back Porch.
   Ⓑ Nana has two Dogs, named Hank and Sugar, who love the back porch.
   Ⓒ Nana has two dogs, named Hank and Sugar, who love the back porch.
   Ⓓ nana has two dogs, named Hank and Sugar, who love the back porch.

3. Select the sentence that uses capital letters correctly.

   Ⓐ "You just missed the bus!" Marrah's mother yelled. "Why can't you ever be on time?"
   Ⓑ "You just missed the bus!" Marrah's Mother yelled. "Why can't you ever be on time?"
   Ⓒ "you just missed the bus!" Marrah's mother yelled. "why can't you ever be on time?"
   Ⓓ "You just missed the bus!" marrah's Mother yelled. "Why can't you ever be on time?"

4. Select the sentence that uses capital letters correctly.

   Ⓐ With her eyes closed, she imagined her Mother helping her get dressed and ready for tonight.
   Ⓑ With Her eyes closed, she imagined her Mother helping Her get dressed and ready for tonight.
   Ⓒ With her eyes closed, she imagined her mother helping her get dressed and ready for tonight.
   Ⓓ with her eyes closed, she imagined her mother helping her get dressed and ready for tonight.

5. Select the sentence that uses capital letters correctly.

   Ⓐ A Person good at sports is usually given preference over others for admission to colleges.
   Ⓑ A person good at sports is usually given preference over others for admission to Colleges.
   Ⓒ a person good at sports is usually given preference over others for admission to colleges.
   Ⓓ A person good at sports is usually given preference over others for admission to colleges.

6. Which of the following words or terms are capitalized correctly?

   Ⓐ I, You, Texas, Katie
   Ⓑ I, you, Texas, Katie
   Ⓒ I, You, Texas, katie
   Ⓓ I, You, texas, Katie

7. Which of the following words or terms are capitalized correctly?

   Ⓐ Winter, Thanksgiving, Bobby, Cat
   Ⓑ Winter, Thanksgiving, bobby, cat
   Ⓒ winter, Thanksgiving, Bobby, cat
   Ⓓ Winter, Thanksgiving, Bobby, cat

8. Select the sentence that uses capital letters correctly.

   Ⓐ Sam's Wife could not resist food.
   Ⓑ sam's wife could not resist food.
   Ⓒ Sam's wife could not resist food.
   Ⓓ sam's Wife could not resist food.

9. Select the sentence that uses capital letters correctly.

   Ⓐ My mother works Extremely hard as a nurse.
   Ⓑ My Mother works extremely hard as a Nurse.
   Ⓒ My mother works extremely hard as a nurse.
   Ⓓ My Mother works extremely hard as a nurse.

10. Select the sentence that uses capital letters correctly.

    Ⓐ The President lives in the White House which is located in Washington, D.C.
    Ⓑ The president lives in the White House which is located in Washington, D.C.
    Ⓒ The President lives in the White House which is located in Washington, d.c.
    Ⓓ The President lives in the white house which is located in Washington, D.C.

11. Select the sentence that uses capital letters correctly.

- (A) "Let's go, Marrah!" Her Mother called from downstairs. "You don't want to be late to school too!"
- (B) "Let's go, Marrah!" Her mother called from downstairs. "you don't want to be late to school too!"
- (C) "Let's go, Marrah!" Her mother called from downstairs. "You don't want to be late to school too!"
- (D) "Let's go, marrah!" Her Mother called from downstairs. "You don't want to be late to school too!"

12. Select the sentence that uses capital letters correctly.

- (A) I wanted to do the right thing for my Aunt Susan, my mother, my father, and the rest of my family.
- (B) I wanted to do the right thing for my Aunt Susan, my mother, my father, and the rest of my Family.
- (C) I wanted to do the right thing for my Aunt Susan, my Mother, my Father, and the rest of my family.
- (D) I wanted to do the right thing for my Aunt Susan, my Mother, my Father, and the rest of my Family.

Do NOT write your answers in this book. To open the answer sheet, scan the QR code or visit **lumoslearning.com/a/5e029**

Chapter 3 → Lesson 8: Punctuation

1. Which sentence has the correct punctuation?

   Ⓐ Will your mom take us to school, or do we have to take the bus?
   Ⓑ Will your Mom, take us to school, or do we have to take the bus.
   Ⓒ Will your Mom, take us to school, or do we have to take the bus?
   Ⓓ Will your Mom take us to school, or do we have to take the bus.

2. Which sentence has the correct punctuation?

   Ⓐ After I scraped the gum off my shoes I went into the house!
   Ⓑ After I scraped the gum off my shoes, I went into the house.
   Ⓒ After I scraped the gum off my shoes I went into the house?
   Ⓓ After, I scraped the gum off my shoes I went into the house.

3. Which sentence has the correct punctuation?

   Ⓐ I have already seen the movie you want to see.
   Ⓑ I have already seen, the movie you want to see!
   Ⓒ I have already seen, the movie you want, to see.
   Ⓓ I have, already seen the movie you want to see.

4. Which sentence has the correct punctuation?

   Ⓐ My sister, who will be fifteen soon is learning to drive
   Ⓑ My sister who will be fifteen soon is learning to drive.
   Ⓒ My sister, who will be fifteen soon, is learning to drive.
   Ⓓ My sister who will be fifteen, soon, is learning to drive!

5. Which sentence has the correct punctuation?

  Ⓐ The boss entered the room and the workers became silent.
  Ⓑ The boss, entered the room, and the workers became silent?
  Ⓒ The boss entered the room, and the workers, became silent.
  Ⓓ The boss entered the room, and the workers became silent.

6. Which sentence has the correct punctuation?

  Ⓐ Please don't sing, until I have the webcam ready.
  Ⓑ Please don't sing until I have the webcam ready.
  Ⓒ Please, don't sing, until I have the webcam ready!
  Ⓓ Please, don't sing until I have the webcam ready?

7. Which sentence has the correct punctuation?

  Ⓐ Although the moon was out, the sky was dark.
  Ⓑ Although, the moon, was out the sky was dark
  Ⓒ Although, the moon was out the sky was dark.
  Ⓓ Although, the moon was out, the sky was dark.

8. Which sentence has the correct punctuation?

  Ⓐ The armadillo which is the state animal, is native to Texas.
  Ⓑ The armadillo, which is the state animal is native to Texas.
  Ⓒ The armadillo which is the state animal is native to Texas.
  Ⓓ The armadillo, which is the state animal, is native to Texas.

9. Which sentence has the correct punctuation?

  Ⓐ I took my backpack with me as I was headed to school.
  Ⓑ I took my backpack with me, as I was headed to school.
  Ⓒ I took my backpack with me as I was headed, to school.
  Ⓓ I took, my backpack with me, as I was headed to school.

10. Which sentence has the correct punctuation?

  Ⓐ Whole milk has more vitamins but skim milk has less fat.
  Ⓑ Whole milk, has more vitamins, but skim milk, has less fat.
  Ⓒ Whole milk has more vitamins, but skim milk has less fat.
  Ⓓ Whole milk, has more vitamins but skim milk has less fat.

Do NOT write your answers in this book. To open the answer sheet, scan the QR code or visit **lumoslearning.com/a/5e030**

Chapter 3 → Lesson 9: Commas in Introductory Phrases

1. Which word correctly completes the sentence below?

   An introductory phrase comes at the _____ of a sentence.

   Ⓐ beginning
   Ⓑ middle
   Ⓒ end
   Ⓓ none of the above

2. Which sentence uses a comma in the correct place?

   Ⓐ After, the class returned from the playground they took a math test.
   Ⓑ After the class, returned from the playground they took a math test.
   Ⓒ After the class returned, from the playground they took a math test.
   Ⓓ After the class returned from the playground, they took a math test.

3. Which sentence uses a comma in the correct place?

   Ⓐ If you, always eat breakfast you will be more successful in school.
   Ⓑ If you always eat breakfast, you will be more successful in school.
   Ⓒ If you always eat breakfast you will be more successful, in school.
   Ⓓ If, you always eat breakfast you will be more successful in school.

4. Which sentence uses a comma in the correct place?

   Ⓐ Until, the whole class gets quiet we will not start watching the video.
   Ⓑ Until the whole class, gets quiet we will not start watching the video.
   Ⓒ Until the whole class gets quiet, we will not start watching the video.
   Ⓓ Until the whole class gets quiet we will not start, watching the video.

LumosLearning.com

5. Which sentence uses a comma in the correct place?

Ⓐ By the way you left your book on the table, in the library.
Ⓑ By the way you left your book, on the table in the library.
Ⓒ By the way you, left your book on the table in the library.
Ⓓ By the way, you left your book on the table in the library.

6. Which sentence uses a comma in the correct place?

Ⓐ Every Christmas, my family travels to Vermont to visit my grandmother.
Ⓑ Every Christmas my family, travels to Vermont to visit my grandmother.
Ⓒ Every Christmas my family travels, to Vermont to visit my grandmother.
Ⓓ Every Christmas my family travels to Vermont, to visit my grandmother.

7. Which sentence uses a comma in the correct place?

Ⓐ After, we all were seated the speaker began his presentation.
Ⓑ After we all were seated, the speaker began his presentation.
Ⓒ After we all were seated the speaker began, his presentation.
Ⓓ After we all, were seated the speaker began his presentation.

8. Which sentence uses a comma in the correct place?

Ⓐ At, the next meeting new officers will be elected.
Ⓑ At the next meeting new officers, will be elected.
Ⓒ At the next, meeting new officers will be elected.
Ⓓ At the next meeting, new officers will be elected.

9. Which sentence uses a comma in the correct place?

Ⓐ Last, Saturday Fred attended a play at the Berlin Theater.
Ⓑ Last Saturday Fred attended a play, at the Berlin Theater.
Ⓒ Last Saturday, Fred attended a play at the Berlin Theater.
Ⓓ Last Saturday Fred attended a play at the Berlin, Theater.

10. Which sentence uses a comma in the correct place?

Ⓐ By tomorrow, morning the train will have reached Atlantic City.
Ⓑ By tomorrow morning the train will have reached, Atlantic City.
Ⓒ By tomorrow morning the train, will have reached Atlantic City.
Ⓓ By tomorrow morning, the train will have reached Atlantic City.

Do NOT write your answers in this book. To open the answer sheet, scan the QR code or visit **lumoslearning.com/a/5e031**

Chapter 3 → Lesson 10: Using Commas

1. Which sentence uses a comma in the correct place?

   Ⓐ Sammy, may I go with you to the mall?
   Ⓑ Sammy may I go, with you to the mall?
   Ⓒ Sammy may I go with you, to the mall?
   Ⓓ Sammy may I, go with you to the mall?

2. Which sentence uses commas correctly?

   Ⓐ If I could play the guitar, like you Wally I would join a band.
   Ⓑ If I could play the guitar like you, Wally I would join a band.
   Ⓒ If I could play the guitar like you, Wally, I would join a band.
   Ⓓ If I could play the guitar like you Wally, I would join a band.

3. Which sentence uses a comma in the correct place?

   Ⓐ Yes, I would like to go to the theme park.
   Ⓑ Yes I would like to go, to the theme park.
   Ⓒ Yes I would, like to go to the theme park.
   Ⓓ Yes I would like to go to the theme, park.

4. Which sentence uses a comma in the correct place?

   Ⓐ No I can't, babysit your little sister after school today.
   Ⓑ No I can't babysit, your little sister after school today.
   Ⓒ No I can't babysit your little sister, after school today.
   Ⓓ No, I can't babysit your little sister after school today.

5. Which sentence uses a comma in the correct place?

   Ⓐ The movie, starts at 7 o'clock right?
   Ⓑ The movie starts at, 7 o'clock, right?
   Ⓒ The movie starts at 7 o'clock, right?
   Ⓓ The movie starts at 7, o'clock right?

6. Which sentence uses a comma in the correct place?

   Ⓐ Kathy, will you drive me to the golf course?
   Ⓑ Kathy will you drive, me to the golf course?
   Ⓒ Kathy will you drive me, to the golf course?
   Ⓓ Kathy will you drive me to the golf, course?

7. Which sentence uses a comma in the correct place?

   Ⓐ I promise, to be home before 9:30 Mom.
   Ⓑ I promise to be home, before 9:30 Mom.
   Ⓒ I promise to be home before 9:30, Mom.
   Ⓓ I promise to be home before, 9:30, Mom.

8. Which sentence uses a comma in the correct place?

   Ⓐ This is the funniest, book don't you think?
   Ⓑ This is the funniest book, don't you think?
   Ⓒ This is the funniest book don't you, think?
   Ⓓ This is, the funniest book don't you think?

9. Which sentence uses a comma in the correct place?

   Ⓐ Yes, I can help you edit your English essay.
   Ⓑ Yes I can help you, edit your English essay.
   Ⓒ Yes I can help, you edit your English essay.
   Ⓓ Yes I can help you edit your English, essay.

10. Which sentence uses a comma in the correct place?

    Ⓐ Beau can I come over, and play video games with you?
    Ⓑ Beau, can I come over and play video games with you?
    Ⓒ Beau, can I come over, and play video games with you?
    Ⓓ Beau can I come over and play video games, with you?

Do NOT write your answers in this book. To open the answer sheet, scan the QR code or visit **lumoslearning.com/a/5e032**

Chapter 3 → Lesson 11: Writing Titles

1. **Select a choice to complete the sentence above that displays the title correctly.**

   My favorite Shel Silverstein poem is _____.

   Ⓐ *Hector the Collector*
   Ⓑ "Hector the Collector"
   Ⓒ Hector the Collector
   Ⓓ None of the above

2. **Select a choice to complete the sentence above that displays the title correctly.**

   Richard just wrote a new short story called _____.

   Ⓐ *My Time in China*
   Ⓑ "My Time in China"
   Ⓒ My Time in China
   Ⓓ None of the above

3. **Select a choice to complete the sentence above that displays the title correctly.**

   My cousin's favorite song is _____.

   Ⓐ *Don't Rain on My Parade*
   Ⓑ "Don't Rain on My Parade"
   Ⓒ Don't Rain on My Parade
   Ⓓ None of the above

4. Select a choice to complete the sentence above that displays the title correctly.

Last week, my parents saw the movie _____.

Ⓐ *Superman*
Ⓑ "Superman"
Ⓒ Superman
Ⓓ Both A and C

5. Select a choice to complete the sentence above that displays the title correctly.

Most newsstands sell issues of _____.

Ⓐ *The New York Times*
Ⓑ "The New York Times"
Ⓒ The New York Times
Ⓓ Both A and C

6. Select a choice to complete the sentence above that displays the title correctly.

_____ is one of the longest novels ever written.

Ⓐ *War and Peace*
Ⓑ "War and Peace"
Ⓒ War and Peace
Ⓓ Both A and C

7. Select a choice to complete the sentence above that displays the title correctly.

Has your little brother watched the movie _____?

Ⓐ *Bambi*
Ⓑ "Bambi"
Ⓒ Bambi
Ⓓ Both A and C

8. Select a choice to complete the sentence above that displays the title correctly.

My science teacher read us an article called _____ yesterday.

Ⓐ *Exploring Neutrons*
Ⓑ "Exploring Neutrons"
Ⓒ Exploring Neutrons
Ⓓ None of the above

9. Select a choice to complete the sentence above that displays the title correctly.

I will use some of my birthday money to buy a subscription to _____.

Ⓐ *Sports Illustrated for Kids*
Ⓑ "Sports Illustrated for Kids"
Ⓒ Sports Illustrated for Kids
Ⓓ Both A and C

10. Select a choice to complete the sentence above that displays the title correctly.

Martha's sister starts dancing whenever she hears the song _____.

Ⓐ *I Love Rock and Roll*
Ⓑ "I Love Rock and Roll"
Ⓒ I Love Rock and Roll
Ⓓ None of the above

Do NOT write your answers in this book. To open the answer sheet, scan the QR code or visit **lumoslearning.com/a/5e033**

Chapter 3 → Lesson 12: Spelling

1. **Which underlined word is spelled incorrectly?**

   The birthday party was <u>wonderful</u>! Everyone had so much fun playing and <u>swimming</u>. The birthday presents were great, but my <u>favorite</u> part was the cake. It was <u>incredble</u>!

   Ⓐ wonderful
   Ⓑ swimming
   Ⓒ favorite
   Ⓓ incredble

2. **Which underlined word is spelled incorrectly?**

   I went for a run this <u>morning</u>. Although I <u>usualy</u> run in the evening, I <u>decided</u> to go in the morning because of the <u>weather</u>.

   Ⓐ morning
   Ⓑ usualy
   Ⓒ decided
   Ⓓ weather

3. **Which underlined word is spelled incorrectly?**

   Sports <u>devlop</u> our character. The players have to <u>abide</u> by the <u>rules</u> of the game. Any <u>departure</u> from these rules means foul play.

   Ⓐ devlop
   Ⓑ abide
   Ⓒ rules
   Ⓓ departure

4. Which underlined word is spelled incorrectly?

A <u>weary</u> traveler stopped at Sam's house and asked him for shelter for the night. Sam was a <u>friendly</u> soul. He not only agreed to let the <u>traveler</u> stay for the night; he decided to treat his guest to some curried <u>chiken</u>.

Ⓐ weary
Ⓑ friendly
Ⓒ traveler
Ⓓ chiken

5. Which underlined word is spelled incorrectly?

So as she cooked the meat, she <u>smelled</u> the rich steam and could not help <u>tasteing</u> a piece. It was <u>tender</u> and <u>delicious</u>, and she decided to have another piece.

Ⓐ smelled
Ⓑ tasteing
Ⓒ tender
Ⓓ delicious

6. Which underlined word is spelled incorrectly?

<u>Frantic</u> now, Marrah lifted her sheets to look under them before <u>droping</u> to her knees in front of her bed. She pushed <u>mounds</u> of clothes out of the way as she <u>continued</u> to search for her backpack.

Ⓐ frantic
Ⓑ droping
Ⓒ mounds
Ⓓ continued

7. Which underlined word is spelled incorrectly?

Katie stood before the crowd, <u>blushing</u> and <u>ringing</u> her hands. She <u>looked</u> out and <u>saw</u> the room full of faces.

Ⓐ blushing
Ⓑ ringing
Ⓒ looked
Ⓓ saw

8. Which underlined word is spelled incorrectly?

They all had wonderful things to say about her song and how proud they were because she kept going even when it seemed like she might give up. She shruged her shoulders and shared a smile with her mother. "I just did my best," she answered.

Ⓐ wonderful
Ⓑ because
Ⓒ shruged
Ⓓ shoulders

9. Which of the underlined words is spelled incorrectly?

Once there was a severe drout. There was little water in Tony's well, and he didn't know what would happen to the fruit trees in his garden.

Ⓐ drout
Ⓑ little
Ⓒ happen
Ⓓ garden

10. Which underlined word is spelled incorrectly? Enter your answer in the box given below.

Then, when I came inside to clean, I realized the kitchen sink was clogged, and the washing machine seamed broken.

11. Which underlined word is spelled incorrectly? Enter your answer in the box given below

Her mother called again, and she could hear the impateince in her voice downstairs. She ran out of her room and leaned over the rail.

Do NOT write your answers in this book. To open the answer sheet, scan the QR code or visit *lumoslearning.com/a/5e034*

Chapter 3 → Lesson 13: Sentence Structure

1. **Select the phrase that best completes the sentence.**

    A group of words that expresses a complete thought with a subject and a verb is _____.

    Ⓐ a clause
    Ⓑ an independent clause
    Ⓒ a dependent clause
    Ⓓ a coordinating conjunction

2. **Select the phrase that best completes the sentence.**

    A group of words that does not express a complete thought, but has a subject and a verb is called _____.

    Ⓐ a complete sentence
    Ⓑ an independent clause
    Ⓒ a dependent clause
    Ⓓ a coordinating conjunction

3. **Select the phrase that best completes the sentence.**

    When Juan studied for his quiz at the library.

    The sentence is an example of _____.

    Ⓐ a complete sentence
    Ⓑ an independent clause
    Ⓒ a dependent clause
    Ⓓ a coordinating conjunction

4. **Select the phrase that best completes the sentence.**

   Miguel loves cars, but he can never find the time to work on one.

   This is an example of _____.

   - Ⓐ a simple sentence
   - Ⓑ a compound sentence
   - Ⓒ a complex sentence
   - Ⓓ an incomplete sentence

5. **Select the phrase that best completes the sentence.**

   Please help your father wash the car.

   This is an example of _____.

   - Ⓐ a simple sentence
   - Ⓑ a compound sentence
   - Ⓒ a complex sentence
   - Ⓓ an incomplete sentence

6. **Select the phrase that best completes the sentence.**

   My father warned us about the dangers of forest fires before he took us camping.

   This is an example of _____.

   - Ⓐ a simple sentence
   - Ⓑ a compound sentence
   - Ⓒ a complex sentence
   - Ⓓ an incomplete sentence

7. **Select the phrase that best completes the sentence.**

   My puppy always chews my slippers.

   This is an example of _____.

   - Ⓐ a simple sentence
   - Ⓑ a compound sentence
   - Ⓒ a complex sentence
   - Ⓓ an incomplete sentence

8. Select the phrase that best completes the sentence.

   The sleepy cat is.

   This is an example of _____.

   Ⓐ a simple sentence
   Ⓑ a compound sentence
   Ⓒ a complex sentence
   Ⓓ an incomplete sentence

9. Select the phrase that best completes the sentence.

   Would you like a cookie, or would you rather have a piece of cake?

   This is an example of _____.

   Ⓐ a simple sentence
   Ⓑ a compound sentence
   Ⓒ a complex sentence
   Ⓓ an incomplete sentence

10. Select the phrase that best completes the sentence.

    Although Jason takes drum lessons, he also plays the tuba in the band.

    This is an example of _____.

    Ⓐ a simple sentence
    Ⓑ a compound sentence
    Ⓒ a complex sentence
    Ⓓ an incomplete sentence

11. **Select the phrase that best completes the sentence above by circling it.**

    A sentence that contains two independent clauses joined by a coordinating conjunction is _____.

    Ⓐ a simple sentence
    Ⓑ a compound sentence
    Ⓒ a complex sentence
    Ⓓ an incomplete sentence

12. **Select the phrase that best completes the sentence above by circling it.**

   A sentence that contains an independent clause and at least one dependent clause is _____.

   Ⓐ a simple sentence
   Ⓑ a compound sentence
   Ⓒ a complex sentence
   Ⓓ an incomplete sentence

Chapter 3 → Lesson 14: Varieties of English

1. Based on the dialogue below, which word best describes Francine?

   Francine: Well, aren't you as refreshing as a cold glass of lemonade on a hot summer day! I'm delighted to meet you! My name is Francine.

   Adam: It is a pleasure to make your acquaintance. I am Adam.

   Ⓐ arrogant
   Ⓑ friendly
   Ⓒ serious
   Ⓓ bored

2. Based on the dialogue above, which word best describes Adam?

   Ⓐ casual
   Ⓑ rude
   Ⓒ proper
   Ⓓ silly

3. Based on the dialogue above, where do you think Francine might be from?

   Ⓐ Europe
   Ⓑ Alaska
   Ⓒ the South
   Ⓓ Canada

4. Which sentence indicates use of dialect?

   Ⓐ Would you like for me to help you paint the fence?
   Ⓑ Abe thought about it, but he changed his mind.
   Ⓒ I reckon I don't have time.
   Ⓓ That's ok with me.

5. **What type of character would use this style of English?**

   "I appreciate you taking time out of your busy day to meet with me."

   Ⓐ a student speaking with a college professor
   Ⓑ two teenage boys watching a basketball game
   Ⓒ a patient talking to his doctor
   Ⓓ a woman talking to her best friend

6. **What type of character would use this style of English?**

   "Yo, I'm psyched that we could do this today!"

   Ⓐ a student speaking with a college professor
   Ⓑ two teenage boys watching a basketball game
   Ⓒ a patient talking to his doctor
   Ⓓ a woman talking to her best friend

7. **Choose the pair of words that correctly completes the sentence above.**

   _____ is always spelled correctly, and _____ is spelled the way the character speaks the words.

   Ⓐ Standard English, dialect
   Ⓑ Dialect, standard English
   Ⓒ British English, expressions
   Ⓓ None of the above

8. **Dialect conveys a character's _____, and standard English does not.**

   Ⓐ accent
   Ⓑ locality
   Ⓒ physical appearance
   Ⓓ Both A and B

9. **Select an appropriate speech style that conveys respect for the given situation.**

   A student speaking to a school librarian

   Ⓐ "I want a book about insects."
   Ⓑ "Give me a book about insects."
   Ⓒ "Would you please tell me if you have a book about insects?"
   Ⓓ "Hey, have you got a book on insects?"

Do NOT write your answers in this book. To open the answer sheet, scan the QR code or visit **lumoslearning.com/a/5e036**

Chapter 3 → Lesson 15: Multiple-Meaning Words

1. **What are homophones?**

   Ⓐ Words that have the same meaning, but different spelling.
   Ⓑ Words that have the same sound, but only have a different meaning.
   Ⓒ Words that have the same sound, but have a different meaning and spelling.
   Ⓓ Words that do not have the same sound, but have the same meaning and spelling.

2. **Identify the correct set of homophones from the following.**

   Ⓐ to, too
   Ⓑ there, their
   Ⓒ sea, see
   Ⓓ All of the above

3. **Find the correct set of homophones from the following.**

   Ⓐ knight, night
   Ⓑ hair, hare
   Ⓒ blue, blew
   Ⓓ All of the above

4. **The underlined words are examples of what?**

   She <u>rose</u> from the water and walked to her chair.
   He handed her a beautiful yellow <u>rose</u>.

   Ⓐ homophones
   Ⓑ homographs
   Ⓒ synonyms
   Ⓓ antonyms

5. **A group of words that share the same spelling and pronunciation but have different meanings is called a _____.**

    Ⓐ Synonym
    Ⓑ Homograph
    Ⓒ Homophone
    Ⓓ Antonym

6. **Choose the set of homophones from the following.**

    Ⓐ gild, guild, gilled
    Ⓑ gate, grate, fate
    Ⓒ toys, boys
    Ⓓ None of the above

7. **The word "brake" has the same pronunciation as "break." What are these words considered to be?**

    Ⓐ contractions
    Ⓑ prefixes
    Ⓒ homophones
    Ⓓ digraphs

8. **Which of the following is the set of meanings for these homophones - <u>sight, cite, site</u>?**

    Ⓐ seeing, quote, locate
    Ⓑ sea, locate, website
    Ⓒ ocean, recite, locate
    Ⓓ None of the above

9. **Fill in the blank with the correct homophone in the right order to complete the sentence.**

    I know this is the correct address! That is _____ house over _____.

10. **Fill in the blank with the correct homophone to complete the sentence.**

    She wanted to _____ this dress and take it home today.

Do NOT write your answers in this book. To open the answer sheet, scan the QR code or visit **lumoslearning.com/a/5e037**

Chapter 3 → Lesson 16: Context Clues

1. **Select the best definition for the underlined word based on the context clues.**

   The snake <u>slithered</u> across the back porch when my mother chased it with a broom.

   Ⓐ stopped
   Ⓑ moved
   Ⓒ slept
   Ⓓ ate

2. **Select the best definition for the underlined word based on the context clues.**

   Our dog <u>gnawed</u> through the rope, allowing him to get loose and leave the backyard.

   Ⓐ stopped
   Ⓑ moved
   Ⓒ slept
   Ⓓ chewed

3. **Select the best definition of the underlined word based on the context clues.**

   Jan took one look at the <u>hideous</u> creature and ran away in disgust.

   Ⓐ very unpleasant and frightful
   Ⓑ beautiful but frightful
   Ⓒ very happy and excited
   Ⓓ very scared and alone

4. Select the best definition for the underlined word based on the context clues.

Emily's mother <u>sternly</u> told her to finish practicing the piano, because she had taken long enough.

Ⓐ happily
Ⓑ beautifully
Ⓒ sadly
Ⓓ strictly

5. Select the best definition for the underlined word based on the context clues.

Her mother called again, and she could hear the <u>impatience</u> in her voice downstairs.

Ⓐ patience
Ⓑ annoyance
Ⓒ endurance
Ⓓ persistence

6. Select the best definition for the underlined word based on the context clues.

He <u>snatched</u> the chickens out of the yard and ran off with them!

Ⓐ stole
Ⓑ gave
Ⓒ smelled
Ⓓ glowed

7. Select the best definition of the underlined word based on the context clues.

Ellen peered between the red curtains and realized she was truly nervous. She couldn't believe this many people were here to see her. She was a <u>novice!</u> Most new performers never had this large of a crowd.

Ⓐ average
Ⓑ experienced
Ⓒ beginner
Ⓓ regular

8. Select the phrase that best completes the above sentence.

Words that provide the definition of an unknown word explicitly stated in the text are considered _____.

Ⓐ inferential context clues
Ⓑ unusual context clues
Ⓒ written context clues
Ⓓ direct context clues

9. Select the best definition of the underlined word based on the context clues.

Keely was bored. She spent each day counting buttons, and she did not believe that there could be a more <u>monotonous</u> task. But even though it was repetitive and boring, she knew it was important.

Ⓐ dull
Ⓑ exciting
Ⓒ advantageous
Ⓓ varied

10. Select the best definition of the underlined word based on the context clues.

My father told me it would not be <u>prudent</u> to eat too much candy at one time. Now that I am sick to my stomach, I wish I had listened to him.

Ⓐ unwise
Ⓑ unexpected
Ⓒ expected
Ⓓ wise

11. Select the best definition of the underlined word based on the context clues.

Sandra was not happy with the way her group assignment was going. She knew her teacher believed in the importance of <u>collaborative</u> work, but it really felt like she was doing it all by herself.

Ⓐ individual
Ⓑ expectation
Ⓒ shared
Ⓓ separate

12. Select the best definition of the underlined word based on the context clues.

The family tree project was almost complete. Sharon finished the maternal side last week after visiting with her mother's parents. Now she only had to worry about the paternal side.

Ⓐ mother's
Ⓑ grandfather's
Ⓒ sister's
Ⓓ father's

Do NOT write your answers in this book. To open the answer sheet, scan the QR code or visit *lumoslearning.com/a/5e038*

Chapter 3 → Lesson 17: Roots and Affixes

1. Which of the following is a true statement?

   Ⓐ A suffix or ending is an affix, which is placed at the end of a word.
   Ⓑ A prefix or beginning is an affix, which is placed at the beginning of a word.
   Ⓒ A suffix is attached at the beginning of a word.
   Ⓓ Both A and B

2. What is the prefix in the word unhappy?

   Ⓐ unh
   Ⓑ u
   Ⓒ un
   Ⓓ None of these

3. What prefix changes the word, 'cycle', to mean "a moving device with two wheels"?

   Ⓐ tri
   Ⓑ dual
   Ⓒ bi
   Ⓓ quad

4. Which of the following words does not contain a suffix?

   Ⓐ lemonade
   Ⓑ resident
   Ⓒ dormitory
   Ⓓ liquidate

5. What is the prefix of the word retroactive?

   Ⓐ retro
   Ⓑ ret
   Ⓒ re
   Ⓓ tive

6. What is the suffix of the word strengthen?

   Ⓐ then
   Ⓑ stre
   Ⓒ en
   Ⓓ st

7. Which suffix would be the correct addition to the word music?

   Ⓐ tian
   Ⓑ sion
   Ⓒ ian
   Ⓓ tion

8. Which suffix would be the correct addition to the word friend?

   Ⓐ er
   Ⓑ y
   Ⓒ ly
   Ⓓ est

9. Identify the root word in the longer word unsuitable.

   Ⓐ unsuit
   Ⓑ suitable
   Ⓒ suit
   Ⓓ table

10. Identify the root word in the longer word <u>uncomfortable</u>. Enter your answer in the box given below.

11. Match the prefix of the below words to its meaning.

Circumnavigate, Geoponics, Macroeconomics, Multitasking

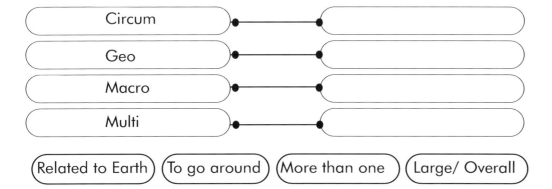

Do NOT write your answers in this book. To open the answer sheet, scan the QR code or visit **lumoslearning.com/a/5e039**

Chapter 3 → Lesson 18: Reference Sources

1. If you want to know how to say a word, look at the _____.

    Ⓐ guide work
    Ⓑ part of speech
    Ⓒ pronunciation
    Ⓓ definition

2. Where would be the best place for her to look up the meaning of a word she doesn't know?

    Zadey is reading a mystery book.

    Ⓐ another mystery book
    Ⓑ the book's glossary
    Ⓒ a thesaurus
    Ⓓ a dictionary

3. In which source would you find this entry?

    marine

    Synonyms: sea, saltwater, maritime, oceanic

    Ⓐ a glossary
    Ⓑ a book about seas
    Ⓒ a dictionary
    Ⓓ a thesaurus

4. In which resource would you find this entry for the word "tissue?"

tissue: a group of plant or animal cells that are similar in form and function

Ⓐ a magazine
Ⓑ a dictionary
Ⓒ a thesaurus
Ⓓ a glossary

5. What resource is this reference from?

abacus (n) Pronunciation: AB uh kuhss
History: 14th century an instrument made from beads and wires that is used to perform arithmetic

Ⓐ a dictionary
Ⓑ a glossary
Ⓒ a thesaurus
Ⓓ a math textbook

6. In what source would you find this text?

kindle: to start (a fire) burning

Ⓐ a pamphlet about camping
Ⓑ a thesaurus
Ⓒ a glossary
Ⓓ a dictionary

7. _____ is a book that contains facts and figures about all kinds of topics.

Ⓐ An almanac
Ⓑ An atlas
Ⓒ An autobiography
Ⓓ A brochure

8. _____ is a book of maps.

Ⓐ An almanac
Ⓑ An atlas
Ⓒ A dictionary
Ⓓ An encyclopedia

9. **Fill in the blank by selecting the correct answer from the 4 choices given**

   You can use a dictionary to learn _____.

   Ⓐ correct spellings
   Ⓑ definitions
   Ⓒ parts of speech
   Ⓓ all of the above

10. **Fill in the blank by selecting the correct answer from the 4 choices given.**

    _____ is a type of reference source that gives lists of synonyms and antonyms.

    Ⓐ An almanac
    Ⓑ An atlas
    Ⓒ An encyclopedia
    Ⓓ A thesaurus

Chapter 3 → Lesson 19: Interpreting Figurative Language

1. **What is the meaning of the simile below?**

   The boys ran off like rockets shooting up to the stars.

   Ⓐ The boys ran toward the stars.
   Ⓑ The boys ran away quickly.
   Ⓒ The boys were shooting guns.
   Ⓓ The boys drove rockets.

2. **What is the meaning of the metaphor below?**

   Dad's business is a well-oiled machine.

   Ⓐ Dad's business runs smoothly.
   Ⓑ Dad's business uses a lot of machines.
   Ⓒ Dad's business sells oil.
   Ⓓ Dad's business is putting oil on machines.

3. **What is the meaning of the simile below?**

   My best friend and I are like two peas in a pod.

   Ⓐ The two friends like to eat peas.
   Ⓑ The two friends are very similar.
   Ⓒ The two friends are like vegetables.
   Ⓓ The two friends live in a pod.

4. What is the meaning of the simile below?

Without my glasses, I'm as blind as a bat.

Ⓐ The person lives in a cave.
Ⓑ The person is black like a bat.
Ⓒ The person is blind.
Ⓓ The person can't see very well without his or her eyeglasses.

5. What is the meaning of the idiom below?

My teacher was as mad as an old wet hen when three kids didn't do their homework.

Ⓐ The teacher lived on a farm.
Ⓑ The teacher was crazy.
Ⓒ The teacher was very angry.
Ⓓ The teacher didn't assign any homework.

6. What is the meaning of the metaphor below?

Nick is a pig when he eats.

Ⓐ Nick eats on the ground.
Ⓑ Nick eats a lot, and he is messy.
Ⓒ Nick has pink cheeks.
Ⓓ Nick makes pig-like snorts.

7. What is the meaning of the metaphor below?

My room is a disaster after my little cousins come over and play.

Ⓐ An earthquake hit my room.
Ⓑ My room is very messy.
Ⓒ My cousins were involved in a disaster.
Ⓓ My room is full of cousins.

8. What is the meaning of the simile below?

I felt like a fish out of water in the foreign city.

Ⓐ I'm a good swimmer.
Ⓑ I'm very wet.
Ⓒ I can speak a foreign language.
Ⓓ I feel like I don't belong.

9. What is the meaning of the simile below?

The little girl was as good as gold at the church service.

Ⓐ She was golden colored.
Ⓑ She wore lots of jewelry.
Ⓒ She behaved very well.
Ⓓ She wore a gold dress.

10. What is the meaning of the metaphor below?

My husband is the apple of my eye.

Ⓐ My husband is one of my favorite people.
Ⓑ My husband looks like a fruit.
Ⓒ My husband has nice eyes.
Ⓓ My husband brings me apples.

Do NOT write your answers in this book. To open the answer sheet, scan the QR code or visit **lumoslearning.com/a/5e041**

Chapter 3 → Lesson 20: Idioms, Adages, and Proverbs

1. What is a phrase which contains advice or a generally accepted truth called?

   Ⓐ adage
   Ⓑ idiom
   Ⓒ proverb
   Ⓓ simile

2. Which sentence is an example of the below proverb?

   Do not put all your eggs in one basket.

   Ⓐ Do not put all your golf balls in one game.
   Ⓑ Do not keep all your information a secret.
   Ⓒ Do not store all your data on just one computer.
   Ⓓ Do not eat all your breakfast at dinner.

3. This famous saying is an example of _____.

   If anything can go wrong, it will.

   Ⓐ an idiom
   Ⓑ an adage
   Ⓒ a proverb
   Ⓓ an alliteration

4. The below sentence is an example of _____.

   She is really rubbing me the wrong way.

   Ⓐ an idiom
   Ⓑ a proverb
   Ⓒ an adage
   Ⓓ a simile

5. **The below sentence is an example of _____.**

   Mrs. Smith's class is going bananas!

   Ⓐ an idiom
   Ⓑ an adage
   Ⓒ a proverb
   Ⓓ a simile

6. **The below sentence is an example of _____.**

   A friend in need is a friend indeed.

   Ⓐ an idiom
   Ⓑ an adage
   Ⓒ a proverb
   Ⓓ a simile

7. **What does this adage mean?**

   Actions speak louder than words.

   Ⓐ Actions make a lot of noise compared to words.
   Ⓑ It is better to do and show rather than simply talk without doing anything.
   Ⓒ What you actually *do* is more important than what you *say* you will do.
   Ⓓ Both B and C

Remember, don't let the cat out of the bag and tell dad about the surprise party for his birthday.

8. **Fill in the blank with a idiom, don't let the cat out of the bag means _____.**

9. **Which of the proverbs given in the choices below means the same as the sentence below?**

   When a bad thing happens, there is always a positive aspect to it.

   Ⓐ Every dog has its day.
   Ⓑ Every cloud has a silver lining.
   Ⓒ A bird in hand is worth two in the bush.
   Ⓓ Patience pays.

LumosLearning.com

10. Which of the proverbs given in the choices below means the same as the following sentence?

You should be happy with what you have, even if it is less than what you want.

Ⓐ Where there is a will, there is a way.
Ⓑ Cut your coat according to the cloth.
Ⓒ Half a loaf is better than no bread.
Ⓓ None of the above

11. Fill in the blank with a suitable idiom to give advice to your friend.

My friend was complaining that he was exhausted from studying the whole day. He asked me what to do. I said, "_____."

Do NOT write your answers in this book. To open the answer sheet, scan the QR code or visit **lumoslearning.com/a/5e042**

Chapter 3 → Lesson 21: Synonyms and Antonyms

1. Choose the set of antonyms of the word murmur.

   The murmur of the stoves,
   The chuckles of the water pipes

   Ⓐ roar, growl, loud
   Ⓑ silent, quiet, still
   Ⓒ silent, roar, quiet
   Ⓓ silent, loud, rumble

2. What are synonyms?

   Ⓐ Words that have similar meanings
   Ⓑ Words that have different meanings
   Ⓒ Words that have the same meanings and are spelled the same
   Ⓓ None of the above

3. What are antonyms?

   Ⓐ Words that have the same meanings
   Ⓑ Words that have different meanings
   Ⓒ Both A and B
   Ⓓ Words that have opposite meanings

4. Choose the set of words that are antonyms of one another.

   Ⓐ return, march
   Ⓑ alive, dead
   Ⓒ opened, broke
   Ⓓ collect, take

5. **What is a synonym for the word <u>rob</u> as it is used in the below paragraph?**

   Once there was a severe drought; there was little water in Tony's well, and he didn't know what would happen to the fruit trees in his garden. Just then, he noticed three men looking intently at his house. He was certain that the three were planning to rob his house.

   Ⓐ cheat
   Ⓑ thieves
   Ⓒ steal
   Ⓓ borrow

6. **What is a synonym for the word <u>intently</u> as it is used in the paragraph?**

   Ⓐ lightly
   Ⓑ watchfully
   Ⓒ attentively
   Ⓓ both B and C

7. **Which words below are both antonyms for the word <u>fragile</u> in the below paragraph?**

   He ordered his servants to collect all the pieces of glass and melt them down and make them into a globe with all the countries of the world upon it, to remind himself and others, that the earth is as <u>fragile</u> as that glass cupboard.

   Ⓐ breakable, delicate
   Ⓑ beautiful, strong
   Ⓒ sturdy, unbreakable
   Ⓓ delicate, unbreakable

8. **Read the following sentence and identify the words that are synonyms.**

   After guests ate dinner, they devoured the dessert with delight.

   Ⓐ devoured, delight
   Ⓑ ate, devoured
   Ⓒ dessert, delight
   Ⓓ dinner, dessert

9. Read the following sentence and identify the words that are antonyms.

The stars appear tiny from earth, but they are actually huge objects in the universe.

Ⓐ tiny, huge
Ⓑ stars, earth
Ⓒ appear, actually
Ⓓ earth, universe

10. Read the following sentence and identify the words that are synonyms.

My math teacher and my gym instructor are good tennis players.

Ⓐ teacher, player
Ⓑ instructor, player
Ⓒ gym, tennis
Ⓓ teacher, instructor

11. Read the following sentence and identify the words that are antonyms.

There is a huge difference between the lowest and highest scorers of the math exam.

Ⓐ huge, highest
Ⓑ lowest, huge
Ⓒ huge, difference
Ⓓ lowest, highest

Do NOT write your answers in this book. To open the answer sheet, scan the QR code or visit **lumoslearning.com/a/5e043**

Chapter 3 → Lesson 22: Vocabulary

1. **Choose the definition of the underlined word in the sentence below.**

   It is difficult to find a movie store that sells video tapes, because video tapes are nearly <u>obsolete</u>.

   Ⓐ very loud and disturbing
   Ⓑ simple to operate
   Ⓒ no longer produced or used
   Ⓓ a traditional story

2. **Choose the definition of the underlined word in the sentence below.**

   If you will <u>provide</u> me with your phone number, I will call you when your order is ready to be picked up.

   Ⓐ make available for use
   Ⓑ leave one's job and stop working
   Ⓒ hold onto
   Ⓓ keep secret and confidential

3. **Choose the definition of the underlined word in the sentence below.**

   It is a wise idea to <u>retain</u> a copy of your receipt when making a purchase in case you need to return it.

   Ⓐ make available for use
   Ⓑ hold onto or keep
   Ⓒ throw away or dispose of
   Ⓓ make a photocopy

4. Choose the definition of the underlined word in the sentence below.

   My uncle plans to retire from the steel factory when he turns sixty-five years old in October.

   Ⓐ hide or conceal
   Ⓑ work additional hours
   Ⓒ clean up an area
   Ⓓ leave one's job and stop working

5. Choose the definition of the underlined word in the sentence below.

   My favorite Greek myth is the story about Pandora's Box.

   Ⓐ a box to keep special belongings
   Ⓑ a family heirloom
   Ⓒ a traditional story
   Ⓓ a writing assignment

6. Choose the word that correctly completes the sentence below.

   The people of the village were tired of being treated badly, so they made the decision to _____ the king.

   Ⓐ budge
   Ⓑ convert
   Ⓒ revert
   Ⓓ overthrow

7. Choose the word that correctly completes the sentence below.

   She pushed as hard as she could, but the heavy bookshelf would not _____.

   Ⓐ budge
   Ⓑ convert
   Ⓒ revert
   Ⓓ overthrow

8. Choose the word that correctly completes the sentence below.

   I need to know where to go to _____ my American dollars to Mexican pesos.

   Ⓐ budge
   Ⓑ convert
   Ⓒ revert
   Ⓓ overthrow

9. Choose the correct answer choice that correctly completes the sentence below.

   When a child no longer has parents, the court will appoint a _____.

   Ⓐ babysitter
   Ⓑ guardian
   Ⓒ monitor
   Ⓓ bookkeeper

10. Choose the correct answer choice that correctly completes the sentence below.

    It is difficult to see on a foggy morning, because it is _____.

    Ⓐ beautiful
    Ⓑ hazy
    Ⓒ rainy
    Ⓓ sunny

End of Language

Lumos Test Mastery tedBook - Grade 5 ELA, Student Copy

Contributing Author - Julie Turner
Contributing Author - Brenda Green
Contributing Author - George Smith
Contributing Author - Wendy Bundgaard
Executive Producer - Mukunda Krishnaswamy
Program Director - Anirudh Agarwal
Designer and Illustrator - Sowmya R.

COPYRIGHT ©2023 by Lumos Information Services, LLC. ALL RIGHTS RESERVED. No portion of this book may be reproduced mechanically, electronically or by any other means, including photocopying, recording, taping, Web Distribution or Information Storage and Retrieval systems, without prior written permission of the Publisher, Lumos Information Services, LLC.

ISBN 13: 979-8868279447

Printed in the United States of America

CONTACT INFORMATION

LUMOS INFORMATION SERVICES, LLC

- PO Box 1575, Piscataway, NJ 08855-1575
- www.LumosLearning.com
- Email: support@lumoslearning.com
- Tel: (732) 384-0146
- Fax: (866) 283-6471

Step Up Your Skills

Also Available

Lumos Test Mastery tedBook - Grade 5 Math, Student Copy

TEST MASTERY
Mathematics
Boost State Assessment Scores

Grade 5

30+ Skills

Student Copy

tedBook

Online Access Includes

- 2 Full-Length Practice Tests
- Answers & Detailed Explanations
- Personalized Study Plan & Resources
- Automated Scoring and Instant Feedback

Made in the USA
Middletown, DE
26 March 2025

73286710R00109